DAVID OF MUSKRAT BOTTOM

TO MARLENE,
ENJOY MY BOOK!

David
of
Muskrat Bottom

Adrian Schaar

David of Muskrat Bottom
Copyright © 2021 by Adrian Schaar

All rights reserved. No part of this book may be reproduced
or transmitted in any form or by any means without
written permission from the author.

ISBN 979-8-9851740-0-7

Book design by Ohio Family Publishing
Cover design by Kathy Bergstrom
Cover image by Brian Cronebach

I GRATEFULLY DEDICATE THESE PAGES TO:

My three amazing daughters
Whose encouragement was the genesis of this book

Brian, Tom and Eric for making my
Daughters' lives complete

My loving wife
Whose encouragement kept me on task
And experienced teacher's eye
Made most of my ramblings readable

Bryn, Seth, Anna, Claire, Camryn and Brooke
Whose lives are a constant inspiration to this Grandpa

Lee Ann Elliot
Whose professional guidance is appreciated beyond "words"
Thank you

My loosely organized group of writers
The "Write Right" Group

Linda and Doug
For their encouragement, suggestions and friendship

Linda, Susan and Jodi at the VA
Thank you for listening

My Son-in-Law Brian for the cover sketch

Kathy Bergstrom of Ohio Family Publishing
For her layout and design skills

AND

Ollie and Chester
My constant companions during hours of writing…
And rewriting

Words form the thread on which
we string our experiences.

Aldous Huxley
1937

'Tis the good reader that makes the good book.

Ralph Waldo Emerson
1803 - 1882

A writer is a person for whom writing
is more difficult than it is for other people.

Paul Thomas Mann
1875 -1955

Honey, please quit writing and come to bed.

My Wife
Recently

*My childhood's home I see again,
And sadden with the view;
And still, as memory crowds my brain,
There's pleasure in it too.*

*From: The Poems of
Abraham Lincoln*

AUTHOR'S NOTE

From the title, you might assume my book is a children's novel – or novelette, given its limited length. It is rather, a collection of memoirs of events that have special meaning to me and, I hope, are of interest and possibly of help to you.

As a child I was fascinated by the Bible stories of David, the shepherd boy, to the point of attempting, sometimes with abject failure, to emulate some of his recorded actions. At the request of my three daughters, I began over ten years ago to record the details of an event that occurred when I was eight years old. That story led to others, eventually resulting in these pages.

The accuracy of the following chronicles is limited only by the acuteness of my aging memory, which is still reasonably functional in spite of seventy-odd years of mental dust accumulated thereon.

For reasons that will become obvious, reference to any individual's actual identity has been omitted, or for the sake of clarity, simply replaced by a pseudonym. The only exception is the name of any famous person whose path I may have crossed.

I beg the indulgence of those readers with a low tolerance for or sensitivity to, profanity. While not excessive, a mild peppering of explicit language was necessary to convey the exact meaning of certain quoted statements, as well as excerpts of uncensored amateur military poetry.

I've heard it said that the desire to write a book is based in an excessive ego. While I'll admit to a healthy self-esteem, I think "excessive ego" is a little harsh. My motivation for sporadically dabbling with my book for the past ten years is, quite simply, to tell my story while I can.

Without further explanation I humbly offer you…

DAVID OF MUSKRAT BOTTOM

Adrian Schaar 2021

INTRODUCTION

The Lord is my shepherd; I shall not want...
Psalm of David 23:1

A JUDEAN HILLSIDE
CIRCA 1025 BCE...

He sensed the escalating fear of those around him as he loaded his weapon with deftness born more of reflex than thought. His practiced eye at once surveyed the complete scene before him, yet focused on the slightest movement as his entire being steeled in preparation to protect those in his care.

His enemy was driven by nature and, more presently, by hunger, when it broke cover lunging from the tall grass at a lamb near the perimeter of the flock. With a confidence gained through experience, the shepherd boy launched a projectile from his spinning weapon directly at the tiny area between the eyes of the charging animal, and in the same fluid motion, grabbed the razor-sharp dagger from the sash girding his waist as he ran toward the stunned wolf.

SOUTH VIETNAM 1966...

Sitting in the darkened building with my back to the wall, the only illumination coming from a dim military issue flashlight, I strained to see the words of the letter I was writing. Sensing movement at the far end of the building, I looked up to see six small figures with weapons strapped to their backs, their single file progress dimly silhouetted against a distant security light.

My heart thudded at the sound of the locked door being forced open with a crow bar. Drawing my .45 caliber pistol carefully from the holster I held it in my lap and sat quietly.

CHAPTER ONE

NEW PHILADELPHIA, OHIO
A SUNDAY MORNING, SPRING 1952 ...

Sitting in my usual spot on the driver-side back seat of my dad's 1950 Chevrolet Deluxe four door sedan, I could see that we had arrived at our church for the morning worship service and Sunday school class; an ordeal that would consume the next two hours of this beautiful day. As Dad turned toward the parking lot, the left front tire made contact with the steep apron and, as on every other Sunday, launched my eight year old body willingly across the bench style back seat, unencumbered by a seat belt and accompanied by Mom's admonition to sit still.

Considering the strictness of current Child Safety Laws, it might seem that my parents were guilty of child endangering until we recall that seat belts in passenger cars did not exist, even as an option, in 1952. They weren't a requirement until fourteen years later when, ironically, I found myself still unbelted and not so willingly, bouncing around in the back of a military aircraft known as a "Caribou" at three thousand feet above a Southeast Asian jungle... but I digress.

****

My early exposure to religious instruction was not completely unpleasant. Even though the finer points of doctrine usually escaped my eight year old grasp, my interest was piqued by the material offered in the form of weekly lesson leaflets handed out by my Sunday school teacher. She was beautiful, which could have been reason enough to be a faithful attendee, but the curriculum was also of riveting interest to my young active imagination – adventure stories about biblical heroes.

Talk about your super-heroes! We learned how some of God's chosen figures like Joshua and Gideon brought down their enemies with seemingly innocuous weapons including, trumpets, oil lamps and torches. And how one of my all-time favorites, Samson, with super human strength and uncanny resourcefulness, wiped out an astounding number of his foes when he weaponized the skeletal remains of a beast of burden - the jawbone of an ass! I was surprised to find that it was socially acceptable to use the term "ass" in this context and proceeded to use the new addition to my vocabulary on several occasions throughout the remainder of the day, until instructed by my mom to desist.

Samson, what a guy! But as hero worship, more often than not, leads to abject disappointment, my fellow Sunday school mates and I found, in a subsequent leaflet that Samson had human flaws after all, and eventually succumbed to the feminine wiles of a woman named Delilah. When I discovered that his moment of weakness resulted in his eyes being poked out by his enemies I made a personal vow, then and there, to find out what "wiles" were and avoid them religiously in my future life.

But on this particular Sunday, as I walked into the classroom, my anticipation was rewarded with an excitement similar to that experienced when finding presents under the tree on Christmas morning. I eagerly grabbed the lesson leaflet that had been carefully placed on my seat by the world's prettiest Sunday school teacher, and stared at the artist's rendition of the story of David and Goliath; finally, a hero with an actual weapon! Although I didn't know what it was at first sight, I knew there was a great story about to unfold!

Our teacher attempted to give us the historical background that preceded the pictured confrontation. A two sheet lesson leaf might have provided enough space to chronicle the precedent activities of David, the shepherd boy, and Goliath, the

Philistine giant, prior to this point in the story, but I'll have to assume the printing company was struggling to stay within budget parameters. Nevertheless, as a class we could have done worse than listen to the angelic voice of our teacher as she provided the essential background to the story.

According to her presentation, David, a humble but talented boy, was about to become the champion of his nation. Through a series of subsequent events and several providential interventions (which were more common then than now) he was to become the king of his people. I found this all well and good, but when would we get to the description of that interesting weapon?

The first frame on the leaflet showed Goliath, sword in hand, glowering menacingly down at David who was looking upward at him with the calm expression of someone who might have already envisioned the outcome of the impending kerfuffle or possibly, as one who simply didn't grasp the gravity of the situation! Upon being quizzed, our teacher explained that David's self confidence was based in his unwavering faith in his God. That made sense to me as I had called upon God for assistance at least once in my young life.

****

On the playground my recess period was interrupted by an aggressive third grader who, having been goaded on by a trouble-making classmate, approached me with a threat to do unspeakable things to me in the presence of my contemporaries if I didn't fight him. Filled with fear at the thought of being exposed as a coward, my first physical reaction was the evaporation of all moisture from my mouth. I closed my eyes and breathed the shortest prayer ever mumbled. I opened my eyes and saw the questioning look on my aggressor's face, which was now planted near my chin, and realized that I was almost a head taller than he. It was now or never. Without another thought I grabbed his right arm and twisted him with all my power into a hammer lock (that I had seen on professional wrestling), pushed him to the ground and held him there. Negotiations and treaty details were completed in short order before I released his twisted arm. When the dust settled I gave immediate, but silent, credit to God for making me cognizant of my height advantage, and credited my own personal strength and new found bravery for proper execution of this handy technique. My opponent and I became mutually respectful associates until our graduation from high school. He went on to channel his somewhat aggressive nature into a locally renowned career as a boxer, and I wasn't involved in another fight until I reached Southeast Asia fourteen years later…

****

At my youthful insistence, the design, purpose and method of use of David's sling was revealed to us. I was so enthralled that I asked for clarification on some of the finer points of sling technique. My teacher kindly declined and directed our attention to the next frame depicting David searching the ground around him for the perfect stone. What? David comes to the toughest fight of his life without ammo? In my eight year old opinion David's overconfidence and maniacal faith were going to get him killed!

The next frame showed Goliath holding his sword over his head preparing to split David vertically, while David began swinging his sling in circles above his head.

Frame three depicted Goliath's charge toward David as the stone was released from the sling by some undetectable slight of hand and assumed a trajectory straight at the big fellow.

Frame four confirmed that the projectile had struck Goliath's over-sized forehead and he began to fall backward, obviously unconscious.

The final frame revealed that David had acquired his opponent's sword and was poised to administer the coup de grace, but as eight year olds we were spared any further scenes of graphic violence. That was fine with me because I never was a fan of blood and gore. Besides, I was already reexamining frame three to determine how the stone was released. (I might add that gratuitous violence and graphic depictions of same, as a self-contained form of entertainment for the whole family, didn't become prevalent until a generation or so later.)

As interesting as this account of David and Goliath's run-in was, the details were just icing on the cake because the author had me at "sling." All through the lengthy church service that always followed the Sunday school hour I was preoccupied with the planning phase of creating my very own historically accurate stone launching device. The minister droned on ad nauseam, and when we were finally dismissed to return to our respective homes, I raced to the car. Assuming my usual seat, I reviewed my plans drawn on the portion of the church bulletin that wasn't already occupied by printed matter in which I had no interest.

Dad drove slower this Sunday than on any other Sunday in recent memory, but we eventually arrived home and I burst from the car and headed straight to my bedroom to change into something appropriate for the afternoon's adventure in weapon manufacturing. Creating my own sling by hand was necessary for several reasons. As this was 1952, one didn't simply go out and buy a sling. It was not a commonly used item and even if available, the average eight year old had no money for frivolous spending. Allowances, to my limited knowledge, were nonexistent in low to middle class households.

As soon as dinner (which was really lunch, but referred to as "dinner" because it was the biggest meal on Sunday) was over, I headed for the garage to gather the raw materials for my project. A veritable cornucopia of things for the amateur manufacturer to use in the creation of other things was housed in that garage and the attached shed.

Assuming that God had my back, because that sweetheart of a Sunday school teacher told me so, it seemed to be a providential moment when after only a few minutes of searching I spied an abandoned pair of combat-type boots in a remote corner of the shed. Although it appeared that at least one of the boots had been occupied by a family of mice or other rodent species, a closer examination assured me that the tenants had vacated the premises, leaving behind the evidence of their recent occupation; not unlike some irresponsible human renters. With only minor hesitation, I removed the debris and prepared to harvest my raw materials.

I've often wondered if exposure to small doses of stuff like the above mentioned debris during my formative years may have had a mild immunizing effect, as I was seldom sick, and had no major illnesses until fourteen years later when I made contact with an unfamiliar bacterium in Southeast Asia.

Each of the dusty boots contained a serviceable thirty-six inch shoe lace, albeit without the little plastic things on the ends, and one long leather tongue of sufficient size to make an adequately proportioned pouch to contain a projectile of choice.

Recalling frames two and three of the leaflet, I estimated the length of David's sling to be about twenty-four inches. However, never having been one to waste God given resources, I decided to use the entire thirty-six inches of each lace. As justification, I felt that I had been handed a mandate to improve upon the design of a weapon that hadn't been updated for some three thousand years.

Brushing aside any further rumination, I reached into my right pants pocket and retrieved my ever present "Kamp King" pocket knife. A poor man's Swiss Army knife, my state-of-the-art tool included a three inch blade, can opener, combination screw driver-bottle opener and leather punch - everything a boy needed to do anything. Under one brand name or another, a pocket knife could be found in the pocket of most grade school through high school boys in the fifties.

A few decades later as parenting skills, self-discipline and personal responsibility eroded, this useful tool became popularly perceived as a weapon possessing destructive powers rather than a tool. As a result, the unrestricted possession of same by youthful inventors, explorers and whittlers was legislated out of public places.

Ironically, I have no recollection of having been stabbed by or having stabbed any of my contemporaries even though we were all usually "armed."

By sharp contrast, fourteen years later I was issued, due to another legislative process, a fixed blade knife known as an M-6 bayonet that fit under the barrel of an M-14 rifle. This combination formed a state-of-the-art evolution of the ancient spear. I was trained to use this somewhat cumbersome, though highly effective, weapon to slash and stab my perceived enemies; a skill that I was thankfully, never required to employ.

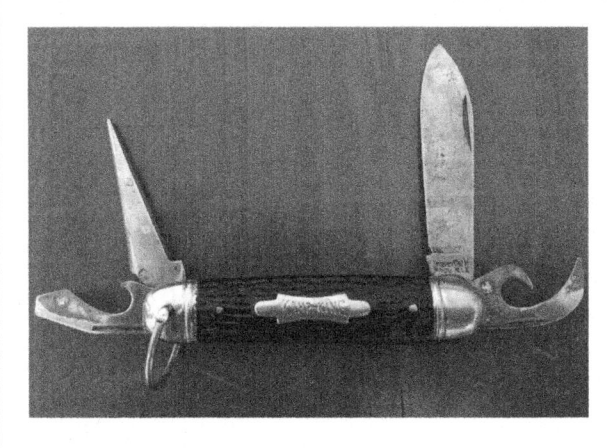

Kamp King knife

****

The excitement of building my own sling was rapidly reaching a fevered pitch, and coupled with the anticipation of using it, justified skipping the research and development phase and getting right to construction. Applying all of the basic eight year old mechanical logic I could muster, I reasoned that bigger being better, my sling would have an oversized pouch to match the increased string length, thereby not only gaining a commensurate increase in power and range, but payload capacity as well.

What was David thinking? Instead of walnut sized ammo as pictured in the leaflet he could have been lobbing egg sized projectiles at his opponents. After a moment's thought, I gave David the benefit of the doubt as I realized that he probably didn't have the historical or equipment advantage that I enjoyed, and gave him credit for doing the best he could with what he had.

Knife in hand, I whipped open the three inch blade and began harvesting my raw materials. The construction phase of my project was accomplished with surprisingly few glitches. The severed tongue of one boot was cut into a shape, more rectangular than square, of sufficient size to hold an egg sized stone. Using the leather punch feature of my tool, I punched one hole into each corner of the developing pouch and one painful hole in the palm side of my left index finger. OSHA guidelines were not in existence until nineteen years later, and probably wouldn't have been adhered to in my one-man enterprise anyway. I loosely looped one end of each string through the two holes at the ends of the rectangle and tied each into a knot. Construction was complete!

CHAPTER TWO

On to the launch site! I had already chosen for the proving ground an area of bottomland no more than a stone's throw from the front door of our house. My own backyard was eliminated as a potential launch site as I had earlier that year been engaging in target practice with a conventional Y shaped slingshot and had accidentally broken the neighbor's garage window.

****

Most of life's significant events, when viewed in retrospect, contain beneficial lessons and this was no exception. My mishap with the slingshot taught me the importance of range safety and the value of a backstop. More importantly, I learned a valuable lesson in human nature. Some people, even neighbors, can be opportunistic creatures and will take advantage of a situation to maximize personal gain. As it turned out I was accused of causing, and required to pay for, every crack in every window in that ramshackle garage even though some of the damage was older than I! To make matters worse, the news of my assumed spree of wanton vandalism spread to the neighbors on the opposite side, and I financed two new windows for them also. It might be of interest to know that when I visited that house and the other neighbor's garage twenty years later, the money had still not been applied to window restoration! Regardless of my opinion as to the fairness of the situation, my dad explained to me the concept of personal responsibility, as well as the importance of maintaining a peaceful coexistence with our neighbors.

My dad, probably the softest spoken, most honest man I

have ever known provided the funding for my reparation to our less than honest neighbors, in exchange for my paid assistance with yard work and general maintenance chores around the house. He thus introduced me, through this seemingly unfortunate event, to the capitalist concept of gainful employment. Another lesson learned! The novel idea of exchanging physical labor for financial remuneration caught on, and I have been voluntarily contracted in various forms of employment and bartering ever since.

****

The assurance of being adequately armed swelled within my eight year old hairless chest as I strolled, sling in hand, down the tree lined tractor path leading to my chosen launching site – Muskrat Bottom.

The tractor path had been cut into the steep side of the hill bordering the eastern limits of the bottomland as an access to the loam-rich tillable earth below. I assumed that prior to being used as a byway for tractors that horse-drawn equipment had been pulled up and down the path. This was evidenced by one of my first exciting discoveries - an old hay rake, probably resting in the same spot where it had been unhitched from its four-legged method of propulsion long before my time. It was inadequately housed in a dilapidated shed, with a rakish easterly lean, that was located near the center of the one-half square mile of bottomland.

On my first trespass into the old shed, I observed the leaning walls, hesitated, then reasoned that if they had stood all this time, and the weather was calm, what were the chances of them falling on me today? With personal safety concerns aside I proceeded into the ramshackle structure. On close examination of the hay rake, my youthful logic dictated that as it sported only a rusty metal seat and no steering wheel or engine, my earlier assumption was confirmed. Its method of movement had certainly been horse power.

A small oval shaped pond was located at the lowest end

of the path. Partially covered with lily pads and other aquatic flora, the pond was inhabited by several varieties of reptilian wildlife and an abundance of muskrats, thus prompting the local moniker "Muskrat Bottom." The seemingly perpetual muskrat population provided a slightly profitable pastime for my step-grandfather, Frank. A local furrier purchased any furs that he could provide.

Frank was the third and last husband of my paternal grandmother, Rosa, whose previous marriages had been dissolved in a time-honored socially accepted way – her former spouses had died. Her second husband was my biological grandfather, Joseph. Frank and Grandma Rosa lived with us, as the practice of absorbing aging parents into the homes of their offspring was more common then than now. That familial duty was assumed by my dad who accepted the burdens and the blessings of life with the same quiet smile.

My brother on the tractor path. The ride down was always easier.

****

My visits to the bottomland were exclusively a midday activity, never dusk, never dawn, as local history had it that an aged neighbor had, several years before my time, walked into the pond voluntarily ending her life. Never having been one to tempt the unknown, I always hurried past the entrance of the foot path that led to the pond's edge on the off-chance that her disembodied spirit might not yet have vacated the area.

The path took an abrupt ninety degree turn to the right around the southeast end of the pond where a land-bridge had been built by successive generations of farmers, each contributing his share of rock, soil and sand, thus damming this end of the pond and providing access over the muddy swamp to the fertile soil that was the bottomland.

As I rounded the sharp bend my bare feet sank sluggishly into the deep sand that topped the path, slowing my progress. As the sun-warmed sand oozed between my toes, a peripheral flash caught my attention. My heart stopped momentarily until I confirmed the source of the flash to be, not a spirit ascending from the pond, but a mallard hen breaking cover. No longer tolerating my intrusion into her domain she scolded me as she passed overhead.

Regaining focus on the matter at hand I wondered if David could have hit a flying duck using his weapon…nah, too small, too fast. For my test target I needed something stationary, something bigger than a duck…yes, the equipment shed!

With no further delay I began the trek westward along the path toward ground zero. As I neared the aged equipment shed, the sand beneath my feet gradually turned into the loamy earth that made the bottomland so desirable for tilling and raising crops.

Stopping about thirty yards from my target, I began searching the surrounding ground for a stone of suitable size and shape for my sling. A fairly smooth stone, the approximate size of what would currently be classed as a Grade A Large egg, presented itself to me about five feet to my right.

As I seated my new found ammo securely into the pouch of the sling and carefully lowered it to my side, it became obvious that the thirty-six inch laces were longer than I was high at mid-body. This new logistical problem faded to insignificance as I remembered, in frame two, David was swinging the sling in circles above his head. All I had to do was overcome the payload's considerable inertia and achieve a centrifugal advantage with my over-sized state-of-the-art sling, and that old shed would be toast!

The first orbit of the payload was awkward, but seemed to self correct by the second round. As each subsequent orbit of the sling gained momentum, the belated question of WHEN to release the payload and, more importantly, HOW, came to mind. My arm began to tire as the loaded weapon seemed to take on a life of its own! Several physical laws manifested their presence precisely at that moment with a reckless disregard for the pivoting anchor point - ME! Gravity dominated the force of centrifugal motion and lowered the orbit of the pouched projectile enough to allow the sling to contact my forehead. The laces wrapped themselves around my head causing the loaded pouch to crash painfully into my right cheek bone!

My first conscious thought, after the impact, was "Am I conscious?" This was immediately answered by the stinging pain that I reasoned would not be evident if I were unconscious. The next question "Am I dead?" was answered by pure eight year old logic as I recalled my angelic Sunday school teacher stating that, "There is no pain in heaven"; thus confirming with increasing intensity, and each throbbing heartbeat, that I was very much alive.

With the reassurance of that welcome thought, my self-centered analysis turned empathetic. Although I knew he was one of the bad guys, I felt a somewhat detached empathy for the historical character Goliath. While remaining fully aware that David's action was completely justified, I realized for the first time the intensity of the pain that comes from getting smacked in the head with a rock.

I was just never comfortable with the thought of anyone experiencing pain. It was some years later and in a different place when I realized pain, whether physical or emotional, is an essential aspect of life, and that dealing with personal pain, or when unavoidable, inflicting pain on others, is no less essential.

Neither was I comfortable with lying, which was my immediate plan to explain the large colorful lump on the side of my head. I rehearsed the various potential scenarios racing through my aching head as I ascended the tractor path to home…"A duck flew off the pond and ran into my head"… Nope… "I got into a fight with a bully, but you should see him"…Nope. I finally decided to just wing it once I got home. My parents were understanding, but protective, and I knew that meant I would not be returning to the bottom, unaccompanied, any time soon.

Upon arrival at home and after giving a truthful, but apparently inadequate, explanation of the circumstances leading to my injury I was relieved of my home made weapon. I was, however, permitted to retain my Kamp King pocketknife as it was still considered a useful tool by my fair-minded parents.

Visits to the bottom were less frequent that year even after being released on my own recognizance, having served a reasonable period of in-home detention known as "grounded." Mom's only condition was that if I was going to pretend to play "David of Muskrat Bottom", I should be more careful.

CHAPTER THREE

By the time my younger siblings were old enough to play outside there was a noticeable change in the neighborhood demographics. Our end of town was experiencing a small building boom with new homes going up nearby and younger families moving in. For the first time in my young memory, kids the age of my little brother and sister were showing up in the backyard to play.

My parents worked outside the home: Mom as a secretary for the local Chamber of Commerce and Dad as a heavy equipment operator. By that time my paternal grandparents had passed away and my maternal grandparents were living with us and had happily assumed the responsibility of daytime babysitters.

Being almost four years older and at least a head taller than this younger set, I was hesitant to join in their activities and instead assumed the role of an advisor and helper - kind of a pseudo-adult. With ages ranging from three to five, their lack of dexterity eliminated the possibility of organized ball games and other sports. Games of tag and hide-and-seek worked, but the go-to game that everyone usually opted for was Cowboys and Indians or Cowboys and Rustlers or Cowboys and anything.

One particular episode of Cowboys and Horse Thieves stands out in memory. The small group chose sides as usual – good guys and bad guys. I abstained. My brother, one of the youngest and not yet savvy to the intricacies of the game, volunteered to be the horse thief as he had always wanted a pony.

A gun fight ensued with cap guns blazing…and one new kid with a squirt gun…squirting. Outnumbered by the posse of good guys, my brother was quickly captured and by unanimous vote of the posse turned lynch mob, was sentenced to hang. A member of the mob was sent to find a rope. It was a lengthy search and by the time he returned with a length of clothesline, attention spans had waned and the group had moved on to other activities.

Not to be cheated out of his hanging, my brother picked up the discarded rope and proceeded to tie one end around his neck. I didn't pay much attention until he climbed up on the porch banister which was not allowed by our parents under any circumstances. He tied the other end of the rope to a pipe protruding from the column supporting the roof. Luckily he held onto the rope as he was pushed off the banister by two posse members, probably preventing a broken neck.

I grabbed him and tried to loosen the rope and yelled for my little sister to get help. She ran into the house, her curly blonde hair bouncing.

She squealed, "Papaw they hanged up Deakie and can't get him down!"

The storm door almost came off its hinges as my grandpa burst through it shouting, "Oh my God! What the ----!" The crisis was avoided and "Papaw" had unintentionally taught us some colorful new words.

****

When things calmed down I thought back to a time a couple of years prior when another incident had played out on the front porch banister.

Having had an obsessive interest in super heroes, I had switched allegiance from Samson, who was dead, to Superman who was modern, strong and very much alive. Drawing on the premise that I was always bigger and stronger than other kids my age, I began to think that I might be related to Superman.

Of course I knew that leaping tall buildings and stopping locomotives were not viable options. However, I could bend stuff like coat hangers, metal rods, tree branches, etc. I also had a sheet that made a serviceable cape.

I was so convinced of my super lineage that I began to question if my parents might have lied to me, and were just waiting for the proper time to reveal my true super identity.

Bending the occasional item became somewhat hum drum, and my thoughts of accomplishing greater feats morphed quickly into thoughts of flying. I donned my cape - a repurposed bed sheet - by tying it around my neck and throwing it over my shoulders.

As I mounted the banister to once and for all prove to myself my super heritage, I looked around to be sure no one was watching, thought a few super thoughts, stretched my arms at what seemed a proper angle for flight and jumped with every ounce of commitment and super strength I could muster...

Less than two seconds and about eight feet later I hit the ground in a full frontal splat that simultaneously expelled all my breath as well as my illusions. My normal breathing returned about the same time as my faith in my parents' credibility.

CHAPTER FOUR

Over the next few years my meanderings in and around the bottom were usually with a friend or two rather than the solo adventures to which I had been accustomed. Prior to this turn of events I could have been appropriately classed as a pre-adolescent loner; the result of growing up in an older neighborhood with no companions in my age group. This problem was mitigated as my sense of community expanded and friendships developed at school and within church youth groups. Some of these new friends were blessed with the enhanced mobility that comes with ownership of a bicycle, and would visit my end of town on weekends; usually to accompany me to the lowland domain that I was always pleased to share.

I don't recall ever asking for a bike of my own, but my parents apparently sensed the need, and on Christmas Day 1955, just a few days before my eleventh birthday, they presented me with my first bike, a green and cream 1955 Western Flyer X53 Super Deluxe with big fat 26 inch whitewall tires. The excitement of that moment was beyond description. The emotional overload was, however, tempered by the realization of what the best Christmas yet must have cost my parents. I was aware of the cost of their gift because a month or so before Christmas I had accompanied my dad to the local Western Auto store, and while wandering around on my own had been attracted to the bike display. Focusing on the very bike I now possessed, I perused the sales ticket and experienced my first ever attack of sticker shock - $69.95! Who could afford that? The sales ticket dropped from my hand as I mused doubtfully that maybe in a few years...I could.

And now that I owned the bike of my dreams and was living one of the happiest moments of my young life, rumination diluted my gift induced high. However, this self-imposed guilt trip resulting from the assumption that my gift created a potential financial burden for my parents was short lived. The sheer beauty of the gift and pride of ownership sufficiently filled the moment to the exclusion of my self-induced downer.

The fact that the bike was a little large for my eleven year old frame posed no concern because I, as well as my parents, knew that the full sized bike made economic sense as it would last through all coming growth spurts; an example of mid 1950's down home logic that proved prescient.

As spring rolled around I began to enjoy the same two-wheeled freedom as my other bike owning friends. We would meet on weekends, at pre-determined locations, for specific ventures or, in lieu of a plan, engage in aimless excursions from my end of town to theirs and back.

Our haphazard two wheeled wanderings in the comparative safety of small town streets of the late 1950's were among those rare win/win situations. It gave our parents a break, was a boon to our overall health through leg muscle development and, not that we cared or were even aware, the environmental impact of our activity was nil.

1955 Western Flyer

****

As spring turned to summer my endless joy riding began to lose much of its original appeal, and in one of those moments of early onset maturity I realized that my bike, in addition to pleasure trips, might be useful in some sort of gainful employment. To that end I applied at the local newspaper office for a paper delivery route. Within two weeks I was the proud proprietor of my own small business with sixty-five customers. As with any well managed business, expansion was inevitable and three months later I acquired another route in a nearby neighborhood increasing my client base to one hundred twenty which generated a monthly income, after expenses, of $36.00...if I could collect it from my customers.

Having previously been a victim of the disturbing tendency of some people to be less than honest in matters pertaining to money, (when I paid for window replacement for the neighborhood) I found myself, once again, experiencing a variation of the same theme – stick the new paperboy with the bill.

Realizing that financial gain was the primary reason for the creation of my small enterprise, I soon developed a collection technique that allowed my fledgling business to maintain a positive cash flow. Simply stated, there was no hour of the day or night that I wasn't willing to jump on my bike and visit some of the more reluctant payers. It soon became obvious, even to my most evasive clientele, that it was more pleasant to pay me on time than to endure my incessant rapping on their door at random, not to mention, inconvenient times; the dinner hour being one of the more lucrative. The overall experience provided a practical base of knowledge and technique for my future career as a banker, but that's another story.

Being built taller and heavier than most boys in my age group, I felt up to the task of carrying the two large canvas bags that were necessary to contain all of the 120 newspapers. With bags stuffed full and strapped crisscross on either side of my body, I mounted my bike daily and wobbled off up the street. What I lacked in Wallenda - like grace and balance I made up for by rapidly achieving sufficient speed for my bike to achieve its own gyroscopic stability.

Delivering 120 newspapers every weekday was an intense physical workout, but Sunday deliveries were a daunting task with twice the number of pages, plus the full colored comic section. Sunday deliveries required a third bag which I perched on the front fender by securing the strap to the handlebars; at best, a recipe for disaster, and probably a fineable practice under government standards had OSHA been in existence at the time.

On one fatefully memorable Sunday, due to the extra weight of the papers, I found it necessary to continually stand on the pedals to achieve the required torque to get the bike up to speed. Regrettably, under the increased pressure, the right pedal snapped off in mid-thrust and a merciless gravity slammed my 11 ½ year old body onto the insidiously designed top tube known commonly as the boy-bar. Why was it a necessary part of a boy's bike if it wasn't needed on a girl's bike? And who was the sadistic, boy-hating Einstein that thought it up in the first place?

In the seconds that passed as my brain processed and passed back to the affected area the inevitable sensation of pain, my thoughts were overtaken with the fear that the external portion of my mid-lower anatomy might have been driven into the bodily region most recently occupied by the lowest end of my esophagus.

After a few long seconds of hanging equally distributed on both sides of the ill-conceived boy-bar, I began regaining my breath amid small waves of composure. As the pain took on a rhythmic throb, I did exactly what has always come naturally to me in these situations. I looked in all directions to see if anyone had witnessed my embarrassing circumstance. Confirming that I was indeed alone and that my most personal anatomical features remained in place, I began to readjust the bags which were now wrapped in a strangle hold on either side of my neck.

As the pain and shock subsided to a manageable intensity, I retrieved the broken pedal and parked the bike where it sat. With no better plan coming to mind, I removed the third bag from the handlebars and started out on foot to complete the deliveries.

Racing on a bike in and out of small town streets, carefully avoiding cracks and curbs and keeping your load in balance, requires focus and attention to the matter at hand – no idle thinking. On the other hand, delivering papers on foot allows more time for thoughtful reflection.

Walking with the additional weight of three brimming paper bags and a waning, although still substantial, pain radiating from the very core of my body, was a challenge that evoked a repertoire of phrases I had learned from my grandfather, but seldom employed. However, once I had walked about two blocks, the pain began subsiding and I reviewed my recent experience.

I congratulated myself on my decision to carry on. After all, it wasn't my customer's fault that the papers were heavy, or that my bike pedal had weakened. They deserved their papers delivered on time. Also, if I had stayed at the location of my mishap, I might still be, literally, belly aching beside my bike. In more cases than not, exercise is a benefit.

Waxing philosophic, I remembered grumbling about the weight of the papers that morning, feeling put upon and thinking, "What could be worse than carrying three full bags of papers?" Life has always answered questions of that nature for me. I learned to quit asking! The lesson learned was - Keep going and be glad it wasn't worse!

The next day a replacement pedal was purchased and installed with my dad's help and I was back on the road for profit as well as pleasure.

CHAPTER FIVE

I always enjoyed introducing newcomers to the more interesting aspects of my bottomland domain. The memory of one boy in particular is more vivid than most, possibly due to the number of hours we spent exploring every nook and cranny of my acquired playground. Though, more likely than not, it was the haunting context of our conversations.

He had a decidedly scientific bent, was extremely analytical, and his youthful philosophy was beyond our years. On one of our Sunday afternoon excursions into the bottom he brought with him, in the saddle bags of his bike, several glass canning jars with lids for the purpose of collecting specimens of pond water. This was the first time we had ridden our bikes down the bumpy path and, come to think of it, the first time I noticed it was bumpy. We braked all the way down against the force of gravity that sucked us toward level ground. Near the bottom of the hill we turned onto the footpath to the pond, parked our bikes and proceeded to the water's edge on foot.

Being always mindful of the history that shrouded this small body of water and knowing that this was the very same path used by the old neighbor lady who had ended her life here, I maintained an intense vigil as my friend dipped jar after jar into the brackish water, and capped them carefully before handing them to me to return to the saddle bags.

His purpose, as it was explained to me, was to observe the contents of the jars for the next few weeks and monitor the development of, uh, whatever developed. I don't recall receiving any detailed analysis of his findings, nor did I request any. I just enjoyed his quirky company and our casual friendship.

Subsequent adventures with my scientific minded friend included riding our bikes to a sand and gravel pit on the west end of town on several hot Sunday afternoons to collect fossils. It was easy picking as most of the excavating of our quarry was accomplished during the work week by the daily dredging operation of the quarry owner which resulted in large piles of clean rock. This activity was more rewarding than most as we each kept our found treasures. Besides, my mom was much more agreeable to the display of fossils on my bedroom dresser than the increasingly odorous pond water from our earlier endeavor.

Our friendship remained casual during the next few years as I began to sense that there was something more about my friend than his obsession with science, politics and religion. He seemed always to be engaged in higher levels of thinking and wanted to discuss his thoughts with me. He always set the agenda of our conversations, and I was perfectly happy with that as I enjoyed his company and always felt enlightened after our Sunday afternoon adventures.

At times though, the conversations took on a more personal, if not uncomfortable tone. Whatever he was attempting to tell me, failed to penetrate the mental fog of my pre-adolescent naivety. He was a year ahead of me in school, which prompted my assumption that he was also a year wiser and, that eventually, I would catch up with his level of intellectual prowess.

During our high school years differing interests led us down divergent paths and we lost contact. Unbeknownst to me our paths nearly crossed in South Vietnam in 1966. We were stationed sixty miles apart as the crow flies – or more appropriately, given our location, as the Caribou flies. I later discovered that he had become fluent in the Russian language in college and worked in the military intelligence department of the U.S. Air Force monitoring Russian radio transmissions in Southeast Asia.

Neither of us had knowledge of the other's military assignments until 1986 when he made a painfully brief visit to my office during his final trip home to Tuscarawas County. He died seven months later in an LA Hospital due to complications from his alternate lifestyle. What my friend had tried to tell me years before in his own esoteric fashion was finally obvious.

CHAPTER SIX

It was April 1962. High school graduation was two months away, but of more importance to many of my classmates was the advent of Class Day – the annual rite of passage for graduating seniors at New Philadelphia High School.

The annual observance, always held the week prior to graduation, included a parade of decorated cars filled to capacity with celebrating seniors driving slowly through the downtown business district. Some were family autos driven carefully by properly attired young ladies and gentlemen with neatly printed cardboard signs proclaiming the occupants' joy at having attained this educational milestone.

Other vehicles that appeared in the motorcade had been acquired by some of the more mechanically minded class members included a motley array of stripped down, fender-less, rusted selections from local junk yards. Some were used car lot rejects that required considerable tweaking just to squeeze by the very liberal safety inspections. In keeping with the questionable condition of the chosen vehicles was the questionable signage that appeared, not on cardboard hanging from the windows, but painted blatantly on any remaining doors or fenders. Some of the verbiage was somewhat daring with one of the more mild examples reading, DON'T LAUGH, YOUR DAUGHTER IS PROBLY IN HERE which, incidentally, didn't speak well to the success of the English Department.

At this point in mid-April my crew of five fellow seniors and I felt an urgent need to acquire a vehicle that would allow us to join in the celebration, yet set us apart from the pack… display our individuality, as it were.

Not unlike the assumed answer to a self-indulgent prayer, that need was met by my Uncle John who had recently purchased a 1953 Plymouth Cranbrook…for the tires! The car was a mess, but the tires were practically new and for $25 he couldn't pass it up. He set to work immediately replacing the bald tires from his work car with the practically new ones on the Cranbrook. Having heard of my search for a car for Class Day he mounted the bald tires on the Cranbrook, drove it the 30 miles to our house and gave me the keys. For the price of a title transfer I had my ride!

The car was a rust bucket…but it ran. The leaf springs supporting the rear of the car were severely rusted allowing its body to rest dangerously close to the top of the back tires. Every bump in the road produced an audible roar as the fender wells made contact with the rotating tires.

Upon hearing of our timely acquisition my pit crew showed up in the driveway, each face beaming with anticipation. The first order of business, by majority vote, was to take a ride. Everyone jumped into the car and the six cylinder flathead engine roared to life. I released the clutch…and the engine stalled. The entire back half of the car, which now contained the combined weight of three teenage bodies in the rear seat, was resting on the back tires and acting as a very effective brake.

The first item on what was becoming a rapidly growing list of repairs was to raise the rear of the car. My cousin Gary, an accomplished mechanic at age 22, instructed me to pick up two '56 Chevy coil springs from the junk yard and meet at his garage the following evening

****

Proudly leaving his garage with a dramatic 36 inch "California Rake," I headed home to pick up the crew for our maiden voyage. All five members jumped in the car, immediately reducing the 36 inch increased elevation to 24 inches which was still adequate to achieve locomotion…as long as no one leaned forward. Leaning forward brought the front edge of the back seat into contact with the exposed rotating drive-shaft causing an unbearable pulsating squeal; not to mention a shower of sparks flying up the pant legs of the occupants. I instructed everyone to lean against the back of the seat thereby resolving the problem.

Next we had to decide on a color to paint our new ride as it had come with an unacceptable faded blue roof and dull cream body. Our minister caught wind of our plan and graciously offered us the remainder of a five gallon bucket of bright orange heavy equipment paint that had been donated to the church in a well meant, but ill-conceived act of generosity by a church member. We politely declined as we had already opted for and purchased a gallon of bright aluminum paint. After a brief discussion as to the method of application it was decided to brush it on as we did not have access to a sprayer.

The absolutely necessary repairs and modifications were completed to the satisfaction of the crew, mostly because our standards were not really that exacting. We enjoyed a certain pride in having broken what we felt was new ground in the art of jerry-rigging. (This tendency has unfortunately followed me into my married life much to the chagrin of my long suffering spouse.)

Class Day finally came, and we found ourselves proudly located about mid-pack in an impressive line-up comprised of 1940's era flat-head Fords, an old truck of unknown vintage, a few non-descript family sedans and one rusty Deuce Coupe with the hood removed to accommodate the occasional squirt of motor oil into the open carburetor resulting in a blinding billow of blue, caustic smelling smoke from the tail pipe.

From the downtown parade we proceeded en masse to a nearby lake where we engaged in an uneventful group swim and an unmemorable lunch before being dismissed back to the school grounds, thus ending Class Day 1962. At worst, the entire venture was anti-climactic, at best, a day out of the classroom.

****

Thinking back, with only minor regrets, my high school years were relatively uneventful. I excelled in the few subjects I enjoyed and barely passed the majority of those I didn't. Several lasting friendships were formed that I enjoy to this day. Some of our teachers maintained only a surface interest in their jobs, doing only what was required to stay employed while others understood the importance of their calling and provided the valuable guidance expected of their professional status.

I was usually self-disciplined, but on occasion quietly rebellious. During those years, prior to being legislated out of existence, corporal punishment was the go-to disciplinary method, and I had the dubious honor of being "redirected" by some of the best, and hardest hitting, staff members New Philadelphia High School had to offer. Surprisingly, I was eventually grateful for their personal instruction and intervention.

****

1962 Class Day Car

Over the next few weeks the Class Day car became my sole means of transportation until I got a short-lived summer job flagging for a road crew. The car began a rapid decline into a state of disrepair which, incidentally, coincided with the increasingly uncomfortable state of self-consciousness I was experiencing from being seen in it. After all, it had been painted to draw attention during the senior celebrations and the celebrating was done...I had a plan. Talking with the local junk dealer I found that if I could drive the deteriorating vehicle to his scrap yard he would give me $50. By this time the starter was shot and the battery all but dead. Not to worry.

I called my good friend and former crew chief to help me push our formerly beloved ride across the road to the top of the old tractor path. It was all or nothing. I had one shot at starting the engine before I reached the soft sand at the bottom of the path. My friend wished me Godspeed and I saluted him in the fashion of a World War I fighter pilot while depressing the clutch and jamming the shift lever into second gear. My friend nudged car and pilot over the crest of the hill and man and machine began the hopefully rapid descent to the bottom. Gaining speed I held the clutch to the floor until the car was even with the pond path near the bottom and...popped it! The roar of the engine almost brought tears of relief to my eyes. It was then I realized that we had not formulated a Plan B, but who needed it, I thought confidently as Plan A had worked. I did a victory donut in the soft sand at the broad spot in the path and began my assent to the top of the hill and my waiting crew chief.

He hopped in, checked for oncoming traffic, and on his signal we burned what little rubber we had left as we headed for the West End scrap yard. With two blocks remaining to our destination the engine hesitated and backfired reminding me that I hadn't considered the fuel level. I punched the accelerator to reach maximum, sputtering, speed and on the next backfire slammed the clutch to the floor and coasted the remaining city block, albeit slowly, to the parking area of the scrap yard.

Never being one to take small blessings for granted, a short prayer of thanks was offered on the way in to exchange the title for my $50. The proprietor handed me the cash with the instructions, "Just pull it around back." I sheepishly explained that it was out of gas, to which he replied through his clenched teeth, "Of course it is."

Having neglected to make arrangements for a ride home

we began our trek back, on foot, to the east end of town. Feeling a minor twinge of something between remorse and sadness as we walked away from the scrap yard, I glanced back at the dusty aluminum colored form with the bald tires. It had served our purpose well. I began to wax philosophic as I considered the limited usefulness of all mechanical creations…and by extension, all beings.

The fate of the Cranbrook was not unlike that of a ship, the USNS Gen. E.D. Patrick, that would five years later carry me and 2,500 soldiers and marines to Southeast Asia, its own usefulness ending in a Naval scrap yard in 1970; just another rusty mechanical microcosm of the circle of life.

CHAPTER SEVEN

Blissfully unaware of the pre-planned brevity of my summer job as flagman for a road crew, I was in the process of rolling up my red flag at the end of my sixth steamy hot day when I noticed a gleaming red and white 1961 Chevrolet Impala streaking toward me in the wrong lane of new pavement. The lane had cooled and hardened hours before, but wasn't open to traffic yet.

My first thought was, "What nut-case had managed to sneak past the other flagman and crew?" As the car braked to a stop in front of me, I recognized the ruddy red face of my employer; one of three brothers who had succeeded their father in ownership of a very successful local asphalt company.

He greeted me with a sheepish smile through the rolled down window of his shiny Chevy with the obligatory, "Howzit goin'?" It was obviously a rhetorical question. I hadn't yet opened my mouth to respond as the main topic of his visit was blurted out. "Uh, we won't need you after today," he said, and proceeded to explain, through my shock-impaired hearing that the foreman's son was returning from college and needed the summer job that, ironically, I thought I had.

As he sped away I visualized my recent plans and dreams also flying away on the new pavement right behind that highly polished Impala; dreams of items to be purchased, not the least of which was a new car.

Slowly recovering from the shock of being laid-off for the first time in my life, but not being one to sulk, I gave myself a mental slap in the face. I had dabbled in minor depression as a mid-teenager and didn't like it. I had faith, based on past experience, that I would find another job. After all, I had been employed since I was eleven.

Call it providence, good luck, or fortunate timing, but by the time I reached home I had received a phone call from my cousin, a bank teller, who excitedly informed me of a job opening at her bank. With renewed faith in my optimistic outlook on life, I thanked her profusely as she explained that the opening was for a messenger. I had no idea what the job entailed, but it didn't really matter as I was fresh out of employment. I called the next morning for an appointment.

The bank must have been in urgent need, as an interview was scheduled for that afternoon. Cautious euphoria would be the most accurate terms to describe my emotional state. I felt excited and blessed with the opportunity to apply for a job with a local bank; especially this particular bank. Founded in 1903 by local industrialist Jeremiah E. Reeves, The Reeves Banking and Trust Company was the largest bank in the county.

****

Entering the bank building through the stately front doors at the appointed time, my anticipation was exceeded only by anxiety. My eyes went immediately to the striking chandeliers suspended from the twenty-five foot ceiling, then down the walls to the marble teller counter which ran the length of the lobby before jutting at a ninety degree angle to the opposite wall. This architectural feature created a spacious "L" shaped area behind the tellers, allowing sufficient room for fourteen desks. Marble floors and counters completed the cavernous rectangular lobby area, which became an unintentional echo chamber repeating the pecking sound of typewriters and the ratcheting clack of manual adding machines.

My darting eyes finally landed on what was obviously a receptionist; a properly attired, kind faced lady with perfectly coiffed, slightly graying hair and a welcoming smile. I approached her desk and managed to mumble that I had an appointment with Mr. J. E. Reeves. Smiling politely, she informed me that Mr. Reeves had been deceased since 1920, but I could speak with the current manager if I wished.

My first thought was to excuse myself and walk right back out through those imposing doors, never to darken them again! However, my desire for employment delayed my action, and her understanding smile assured me that my lack of finesse would remain our little secret. I waited nervously as she went for the manager.

I was still reeling from the thought of the receptionist's first impression as the manager materialized in front of me with right hand extended. I grasped his hand immediately, causing myself further consternation as my mind raced silently, "Did I grip too firmly or was it too wimpy? Oh my God, I think I released too quickly...stop it!" He introduced himself, and before I could think of my name, I forgot his! Thankfully, this latest twitch of anxiety was alleviated as he offered me a seat at his desk where I sat down immediately in front of his gold framed name plate, and the interview began.

Asked to review any work experience, I began reciting a list of jobs, the sum of which represented continual part-time employment during my school years, beginning in the fifth grade, and culminating with my most recent, albeit abbreviated, career move as a flagman.

The manager seemed impressed which I interpreted as a signal to relax a little. The remainder of the interview consisted of questions that were, in subsequent years, legislated out of the interview process through rulings initiated by the Equal Employment Opportunity Commission.

Those questions went something like this: "Will you be going away to college? Are you engaged or do you have a steady girl friend? Are you planning on marriage in the next few years? If so, are you planning a family? With what church are you affiliated?"

Reading between the lines, I began to assume they wanted someone who would be with them long enough to justify the bank's investment of valuable training time, which seemed reasonable to me.

The next thought that crossed my mind was that the

requirements of the job could be adequately satisfied by a faithful, uneducated eunuch with a religious bent...but that was just my mind doing what it usually does to ease stressful situations.

As the zenith of the "ME" generation was still a few years in the future, I didn't think of, let alone ask, any questions regarding vacation pay, sick pay, personal days or health insurance. I was simply glad to be employed!

To make a long story short, the following Monday I began the job that lasted, with one notable intermission, for the next forty-one years. I have to assume that my youthful work record was the determining factor in the decision to hire me, because God knows I had no other glowing qualifications.

Reeves Banking and Trust Company Dover, Ohio

Starting at the bottom of the pecking order as a messenger/stock boy, provided the opportunity to learn the business literally from the bank's ground floor/basement up. Promotions and raises came at a satisfying pace. Responsibilities increased and I was appointed to officer in charge of operations, and in due time I joined the growing herd of bank Vice Presidents, culminating in the position of lending officer and manager of our bank's main office.

Possibly due to an innate inability to delegate, or an overactive work ethic, I found myself, even as manager, still unloading the occasional delivery truck, and checking the parking lot each morning for the prior evening's beer bottles and assorted debris from the surrounding bars.

CHAPTER EIGHT

During the personnel orientation on my first day of work, I was happy to be informed that my duties would include making several trips each day among four of our local banking offices to bring counter work and documents to the main office processing center. Of far more immediate importance to me, I was told a vehicle was being purchased for my use. In addition the new car would be my transportation to and from work. The timing was perfect as I had just disposed of the faithful, but disintegrating Cranbrook. Thoughts of driving to work in a sporty 1962 something danced freely in my mind. The euphoria continued, dampened only by the unsettling thought that I might be dreaming.

The inevitable return to reality came the following day as I walked from the bank to the nearby American Motors dealership to pick up the car. My new ride had been wisely selected by the very conservative top echelon of the bank. The salesman handed me the keys and accompanied me to ... a dull green 1962 Nash Rambler station wagon.

My childish disappointment was short lived as I mentally reviewed my fortunate circumstance. What other eighteen year old high school graduate walked into a new job yesterday and was presented with a new car today?

Although the lackluster station wagon had none of the sporty attributes that I found desirable, it provided me with something far more deviously satisfying. Driving my newly acquired wheels home after work, I allowed myself to engage in a demonstration of latent adolescent ego by parking in the most conspicuous spot in the driveway where it would be impossible not to attract the attention of the neighbors.

It wasn't that I valued their opinion of me, which I always sensed was based on their erroneous assumption that I had been a window breaking vandal. I just desperately wanted to flaunt my unanticipated success in the collective face of their low expectations. At least that is how I rationalized my vengeful display.

Second guessing my decisions and over thinking situations had always been my method of operation and in reconsidering my reasons for acting in a manner so foreign to my character the whole scene turned sour. I recalled, in a somewhat paraphrased fashion, a verse from a Biblical proverb: "Haughtiness goeth before the fall," and I wasn't about to set myself up for any self-inflicted embarrassment.

Acting on this personal epiphany I moved the new car to a less conspicuous spot beside the garage, set aside my contentious feelings for my neighbors and joined my family for a pleasant evening meal, unencumbered by that shroud of vengeful thoughts.

****

As beneficial as it was to drive to and from work in the company car, I was still borrowing the family car for all personal ramblings. It was definitely time to get my own wheels.

For about a week I had my eye on a recently traded '53 Chevy Belaire that was sitting on the discount lot of Weaver Auto Sales just two blocks from the bank. $395 was the price scrawled across the windshield. It was a deal too good to pass up! Besides, the salesman I talked with said it ran like a sewing machine. I assumed that was good. On the positive side, his statement provided me with one of those life lessons that only come from experience: Don't make assumptions based on the claims of a salesman.

With hands in my empty pockets I approached Dad for a $395 loan with a four month interest free payback. Dad's only question regarded the salesman's allusion to a sewing machine. I responded that I was sure he was referring to the smooth, quiet operation of the car. To the salesman's credit, the muffler did work flawlessly. The gear shifting mechanism, as I would soon discover, did not.

Manual transmissions with the gear shifting lever mounted on the steering column were innately problematic, especially if they had experienced hard, careless use under a former ownership.

I was not going to admit ignorance of automotive principles nor concede defeat to an errant mechanical device. Being somewhat mechanically inclined, (in the jerry-rigging sense of the term) I devised a questionably expedient method of realigning the lever extensions when they randomly exceeded operating parameters, causing binding during gear changes. When the malfunction occurred I would lift the hood, stretch painfully over the left fender to access the bound levers, and twist them back into alignment. Greasy fingers being one of the undesirable side effects of the repair, I acquired several pairs of gloves and kept them handy in the dashboard glove box, thus using that convenient storage area for its original intended purpose.

The frequency of the problem was reduced by very slow, deliberate shifting of the column mounted lever from first to second gears; a ritual that took far less time to perform than the default ritual of manual realignment.

The next four months passed largely unnoticed as most of life unfortunately does. My installment loan from Dad was repaid and the '53 Chevy, with its persistent, but manageable mechanical issues, was mine. Strict adherence to gentle driving practices had eliminated the need for the inconvenient roadside repairs.

****

On an uncommonly warm day the following spring, I arrived home from work at the same time as Dad, who greeted me with a broader than usual smile on his dust and tar streaked face. Dad operated the asphalt mixing plant for the same company that had employed me for six days the previous year.

Operation of the aptly named "Hot Mix" plant was a hot, dirty job on the best days, and nearly unbearable during most of the summer months. If his working conditions bothered Dad we never knew. He was not one to complain or share his burdens.

On this day I could see, through the grime, a happy man with good news to share. We hadn't reached the back door when he blurted out that his boss (my former boss) had stopped by to tell him he was selling his '61 Chevy Impala and wanted to know if I would be interested. I had admired that car since the day he drove it up to my worksite to fire me. Putting bad memories aside, my thoughts turned to the facts at hand. The price was well below market value, the mileage was low and the condition immaculate. This guy was a car lover and babied every vehicle he owned. According to Dad the boss had ordered a 1963 Corvette Stingray Coupe.

1961 Chevy Impala (Red, White & Beautiful)

But why me? He could have sold his car to anyone, and probably for more money. Was he feeling bad about cutting my employment short to accommodate another employee's son? Was he showing appreciation to Dad for being a faithful employee? The rhetorical questions faded rapidly from mind as the thought of cruising the roadways of Ohio in that sporty Chevy with the 348 cubic inch engine filled my entire being.

Shortening a long story, Dad cosigned a loan with my bank for the purchase price and I had a dream car. Uncounted hours of blissful joy riding, washing and waxing filled all my free time during the following months. Happiness came easily in those days.

CHAPTER NINE

My elation at having landed a good job with a respected employer and being well endowed with vehicles continued unabated for several months. Then came a letter from the U.S. Department of Selective Service, a follow-up to my having registered for the military draft when I turned eighteen. The letter, in the assuming tone common to official government correspondence, included a pre-scheduled date and time for reporting to the induction processing center in Cleveland. This appointment, the letter stated, would determine my physical eligibility to serve in the armed forces of the United States.

With mixed emotions I boarded the chartered bus on the appointed date, along with a contingent of forty other young men from several nearby communities. Upon arrival at the processing center we were herded inside to begin a battery of routine physical examinations.

All went well at the stations set up for blood pressure, heart rate, eye, ear, nose and throat examinations. These were followed with a cursory hernia check by a distracted looking Army physician. Next was our first interactive exam wherein we were instructed to face the wall, drop our pants and bend over. An unenthusiastic Army medical assistant who had apparently drawn the short straw for duty that day, passed behind us shining an intense light at our collective posteriors looking for, as it was later explained, evidence of parasitic insects. While the test was a bearable affront to personal modesty it did not engender the personal stress I was about to experience during the final exam…the urinalysis.

Presented with a specimen cup and instructed to take a place in one of several lines that were forming in front of, and awaiting access to, a wall of eight open urinals all of which lacked privacy panels, I found my way to the middle of one of the eight lines and stood shoulder to shoulder with at least one hundred cup bearing peers. And then it happened... or rather, didn't happen.

The medical term is paruresis. The non-medical term is bashful bladder, an inconvenient, non-life threatening inability to urinate in a crowd, or on command. Maybe it is a result of my somewhat modest, small town upbringing, but I simply never considered urinating as a social event. Of necessity, the symptoms subsided during basic training.

I stood before the urinal, specimen cup in hand, my mind urging my body to secrete just a drop or two...nothing. The guy behind me, a friend I had known since the first grade, sensing that I was taking more than a reasonable time to complete my assignment, asked me what the hold-up was. I whispered to him, "I can't pee," to which he replied, "We can't stand here all day. Give me the damned cup!" He filled the small specimen cup to near capacity and handed it back to me. While grateful for his help, I silently questioned his excessive generosity, as well as his ability to estimate the amount of liquid that constitutes a specimen.

I walked carefully to the next station gingerly holding the cup containing my ill-gotten sample and handed it slowly to the assistant who gave me a disgusted look that could only be interpreted as, "Really?"

It is with a mild sense of irony that I view the close lifelong friendship that I have enjoyed with my benefactor, while acknowledging that I went to Vietnam on his urinalysis, and he stayed home!

CHAPTER TEN

I resumed my duties at the bank the next day and life was good until September, when the love of my life went out of state to Anderson College. Attempting to fill what was shaping up to be a lingering void, and to improve my chances for advancement at the bank, I enrolled in night classes at the local branch of Kent State University.

As an actual local campus would not be developed until years later, the classes were offered at New Philadelphia High School, four evenings per week after regular classes were dismissed. The curriculum included all classes necessary to complete a freshman year. However, the long work days and night time studies became a drag. In the same manner as a pain remedy provides temporary relief for a headache, but does nothing to eliminate the cause, filling the void created by the absence of my girlfriend by extending my active work day became, at best, a tiresome temporary solution.

After many months of this routine, a growing frustration crept into my daily life. I couldn't continue attending classes on more than a part-time basis while maintaining full time employment at the bank, and of further concern, with no qualifying military deferment, I felt myself ripening daily for the inevitable draft. With the looming possibility of being called to serve my country becoming more of a reality, a stressful urgency was added to my mental deliberations.

Being honest with myself, I realized the situation contributing the most stress to my young life was categorically emotional. I was, much like Charlie Brown of "Peanuts" fame, gloriously and miserably in love with the little red haired girl from my teens; "glorious" because all true love is, and "miserable" because the focus of my attention was now attending college in a neighboring state and would do so for nine months out of twelve for the next three years.

My True Love

For better or worse, emotion has more often than not, trumped logic in most of my life altering decisions. It usually worked out for the best, and when it didn't I accepted responsibility for my choices and worked through them.

Satisfied that I had reached a reasonable compromise between logic and emotion, the decision was made...I was joining up! Enlisting in the military to avoid being drafted into the military may seem counter intuitive, but I had a plan.

Before committing to that plan, I engaged in a month long review of my reasoning, pro and con. On the positive side, neither time nor finances would allow me to become a full time student, and the military offered educational benefits that rivaled a full ride scholarship. With two years banking experience to my credit, enlisting in the U.S. Army Finance Corps seemed a reasonable direction for me. Additionally, the Army's voluntary enlistment period is three years, which coincided nicely with the projected period of absence from the girl I loved and her graduation from college. In the meantime I could compile college credit at the expense of the Army while fulfilling my military obligation.

On the other hand, there were rumblings from Southeast Asia that were sounding very much like the beginning of a war, raising the question…If the Army needed full time combat soldiers, would it honor our contract to give me a shot at the finance corps? To his credit, my recruiter was honest and up front when he told me, "You will be expected to be a soldier first and a participant in your Military Occupational Status second."

My daily mental reviews allowed equal time to the less desirable attributes of my pending action. As a child I reveled in war games; sneaking up on pretend enemies, belly crawling across the back yard, shooting our way out of ambushes with cap guns and setting up camp while planning the next attack. It was the stuff of dreams.

However, considering military service as an almost twenty year old, with the very real possibility of camping out on other than a sunny day, belly crawling on other than soft green grass to avoid detection and incoming fire, shooting guns with real bullets and being shot at with same, was cause for concern.

I can honestly say that the concern I felt was not based in a fear of finding myself in a combat situation. I assumed, maybe naively, that I would be well trained and receive all necessary gear to survive. In addition I was blessed to grow up having a close relationship with several respected uncles who had survived intense combat, and were decorated accordingly, in both World War II and Korea, and one macho cousin who wouldn't know fear if it crept up on him on a dark stormy night.

While I held no illusions that I might be heir to a genetic predisposition toward heroism (I got over that early in life when I proved to myself that my family tree did not include Superman), I was greatly encouraged by an attitude of, "If they did it, I can do it."

Of greater concern at the moment was the idea of committing the next three years of my life to a course of action with no option for redress. Viewed from the perspective of a young person anticipating his future, three years is a much longer time than when viewed from the mature perspective of an older person looking back on a life lived. It's simply a matter of current perspective.

After a month of weighing the pros and cons of my intended action, I admitted to myself that this prolonged analysis was simply justification for what was actually procrastination. The decision had been made a month ago!

Irritated by my own inaction, I resolutely walked into the recruiter's office on my lunch break and signed up. That was on a sunny June day in 1964. The actual date of enlistment was set for October 14, 1964.

On that date, after the proper good byes and good lucks were observed, another life-long friend drove me to Cleveland where I boarded an over-night train to Fort Knox, Kentucky to begin fulfilling my three year military obligation.

CHAPTER ELEVEN

The first painful jerk on my chain of military commitment came at 4am on the first day of training when an overachieving member of the training cadre slammed open the barracks door, flipped on the lights, kicked a large metal trash can between the two long rows of cots and shouted in an unnecessarily harsh tone, "Alright ladies, drop your cocks and grab your socks. Formation is outside in ten minutes…and you WILL be there!"

As our nemesis stormed out the door to his next platoon of sleeping victims, a naïve, but sincere question was voiced in a nasally southern twang by a sleep drugged recruit several cots away, "Should we wear our boots too or just our socks?" Most of us opted for full fatigue uniform.

Standing in formation less than ten minutes later, shivering in the early morning chill of mid-October, we received our first verbal drill order. In the vernacular of the training cadre, which incidentally adds an extra syllable to most single syllable words when shouted as a command, came the drill sergeant's order, "LAY-UFT FACE!"

Most turned left, some turned right as the inevitable question came from that same innocent recruit with the nasal twang, "Your left or ours, Sergeant?" The response emanating through clenched teeth was immediate, "Your military left, you assholes!" For the next hour we practiced differentiating our military left from our military right.

Early in our training the instruction periods included a rather detailed class in Combat First Aid. The first technique to be mastered was the proper method of administering initial treatment to a comrade with a sucking chest wound; a gurgling, bubbling, bloody gash in the chest area that I hoped to never encounter. I did, however, dutifully memorize the details of the technique anyway, just in case.

The training seemed to be an extension of my high school health class, but taught with a more pressing urgency as the potential for applying the newly acquired skill was rife with possibility as our country's military involvement in Southeast Asia was escalating.

Our afternoon instruction provided an ironic contrast as we began learning basic bayonet techniques, including how to inflict a sucking chest wound on the person of our "enemy du jour" should the need arise.

CHAPTER TWELVE

The most ineffectual Army imaginable would be the one that respects the individuality of its members and requests, rather than demands obedience to superiors. A military organization is neither a democracy nor a republic.

Young men and women who are products of our free society have enjoyed, since birth or naturalization, the attendant individual rights and privileges associated with that freedom. Being drafted or volunteering for military service can be the most dramatic paradigm shift many of those young Americans have experienced since exiting their mother's wombs.

In swearing the Oath of Enlistment, the new recruits agree to the suspension of those familiar personal freedoms for the duration of their service commitment. It is intended for the new soldier to become a contributing member of a regimented group of his peers, with the only remaining individuality being an individual responsibility to do his duty as his superiors determine. The essence of basic training, other than teaching how to kill an enemy while staying alive, is to weed out those recruits who cannot adjust to the disruption of their accustomed life style.

One such trainee (I'll remember him as Private Smith) committed a seemingly minor infraction by flipping a cigarette butt onto the drill field. The prescribed, yea mandated, military method for disposal of a cigarette, once most of the carcinogens have been inhaled, is to grind the unburned tobacco between finger and thumb thus dispersing the organic shreds on the surrounding ground then wadding up the remaining paper and filter and placing same in a pocket of choice for later disposal in a proper waste container. This procedure is known as field stripping.

Flicking the butt would have remained a minor infraction,

punishable by a few compulsory push-ups, had he not refused an order from the drill sergeant to pick it up. Disobedience of an order from a superior, which at this stage of our training was just about anyone but us, was an intolerable act.

Private Smith was ordered to assume the "dying cockroach" position, lying on his back with arms and legs stretched to the sky. This did not seem bad at first, but as the morning and our drill instruction dragged on, the blood flow to his vertically extended extremities eventually succumbed to the ever present force of gravity, and he began to complain. Complaining is also an infraction. Private Smith was assigned KP (Kitchen Police) duty for the entirety of the following week.

KP duty is shared on a rotating basis by all recruits and consists of general kitchen chores as assigned by the cook in charge. When assigned as a punishment, the job is limited to the back breaking scrubbing and scouring of a perpetual stream of pots and pans. Removal of cooking greases and baked-on starches is the challenge. Shiny, streak-free metal is the goal. The goal is attained by carefully scrubbing, and rescrubbing, in the event that the item fails to pass the cook's inspection.

Being one of only a few college graduates in our platoon, Private Smith had a superior air when dealing with his superiors; not an advisable attitude to assume in a military environment. I'm confident that his IQ dwarfed that of our drill sergeant, but common sense and decorum were not his strong points. Unfortunately for all of us he had a plan to save face and get even.

He had been drafted shortly after graduating from college where he had observed the method of operation of the fledging protest movements wherein grievances and opinions were aired in dramatic fashion. In keeping with that line of reasoning I'm sure he felt that observing the chain-of-command requirement was for the lesser intellects. He would launch a personal protest where it would get the greatest result. He circumvented the established chain of command and went straight to the Chaplain!

CHAPTER THIRTEEN

The Chaplain was a kind-hearted, gentle soul who had only one flaw; he took action after hearing only one side of the story. Apparently having a slow day, he grasped onto Private Smith's lament, and clearing his slate for the day, headed for a talk with our Company Commander, who immediately called in the Executive Officer, who barked the problem to the Senior Training Officer, who chastised our Head Training Sergeant for allowing the trainee to be so harshly disciplined by members of his staff.

This series of events is a prime example of proper use of the Chain of Command, and in this case, is in keeping with the often used military axiom, "Shit flows downhill." I'm certain that none of the officers cared about the causative event as long as the Chaplain was placated and the problem was off their respective desks.

The flowing feces stopped for a fleeting moment on our training sergeant's desk, just long enough for him to change the direction of the flow from its intended recipients (his staff) to the person who ratted them out.

****

For late October, the weather was uncommonly hot as we returned to the barracks from a long day of training. We were greeted by the stern but smiling face of our training sergeant. He rarely smiled. Vengeance is often preceded with a sarcastic smile. I detected a sinister curl in his lip as he reminded us of our lowly rank by comparing our position as being somewhere below the level of whale shit; then proceeded to explain the gravity of Private Smith's actions, as well as the gravitational direction of feces.

Standing at attention we received the news of Private Smith's talk with the Chaplain. Through clenched teeth, in a tone of feigned sincerity, the training sergeant began to speak. "Men, I had no idea that the members of 5th Platoon were such a religious minded group of recruits, and I want to personally thank Private Smith for making me aware of this fact by his recent visit to the battalion chaplain. Accordingly, I have made arrangements for 5th Platoon to attend revival services at a nearby church beginning tonight and lasting the entire week. The church is located just five miles from base, a reasonable march for men as fit as you. The uniform will be Class A Dress."

His voice then took on the harsh tone to which we had become accustomed, "Get chow, hit the showers and have your uniformed asses back here ready to march in one hour. DIS-MISS!!!"

Private Smith was spared instantaneous mob retribution solely due to the lack of time.

Fed, showered and dressed in our warm wool Class A Dress uniforms, we stood in the hot afternoon sun ready to march to church.

CHAPTER FOURTEEN

From the moment the preacher stepped up to the pulpit we, and the regular congregation of faithful attendees, were bombarded with "fire and brimstone" at a decibel level that would have made our drill sergeant cower with inadequacy, had he been there. The evangelistic barrage was to continue unabated for one hour and thirty minutes with only a moment's cease fire at irregular intervals while the evangelist gulped water from what seemed to be a perpetually filled glass housed inside the pulpit. Within moments of each slurp, giant beads of sweat appeared on his broad forehead only to be mopped away with an increasingly saturated handkerchief, withdrawn from and replaced in, the sweat stained breast pocket of his suit coat.

I dared an occasional glance at our training sergeant who was standing stiffly at parade rest position, sharp as a tack in dress and demeanor, not a drop of sweat evident. As the service dragged on and the platoon became fidgety, I could see a look of satisfaction cross his otherwise stone face. His only discernable motion was to move silently behind the bobbing head of any platoon member who had allowed himself to succumb to the heat of the building and the drone of the preacher, for the purpose of administering a sharp poke with his knife-like index finger to the back of his sleeping victim's neck.

Nodding-off wasn't an option, but as my usual sharp hearing lapsed into an environmentally acquired deafness my mind followed suit, allowing a state of reverie to remove my conscious self from the uncomfortable proceedings. In the same manner as an external sound experienced during sleep will direct the course of a dream, the evangelist's frequent reference to the Lord's name, spoken with that extra syllable (as in Je-uh-sus), piqued my semi-conscious memory, whisking me back to a similar church service, also a forced attendance, when I was about eight years old.

****

It was the same type of church service; a week-night revival meeting with a guest evangelist whose claim to fame was that he had, according to his advance advertising, memorized the entire Bible. The thought of anyone memorizing a literary work of this magnitude was beyond fascinating to my eight year old mind. At age six, I had memorized the lines for my role in a first grade play, and was awestruck to think that anyone could memorize a whole book! My parents had no problem getting me to church on that first night. I had my Bible in hand, a fairly rare occurrence, but not unprecedented. I was prepared to follow along as the preacher quoted scripture from memory.

As the service progressed, I became increasingly disappointed as I had expected him to start at Genesis Chapter 1 and proceed through Revelations. At the realization that the service was not going according to my expectations, I formulated a plan to save what was left of the evening.

The preaching finally came to an end, and the congregation formed a line to observe the social amenity of shaking hands with the minister as we exited the church. As I offered my hand the minister said, "I'm glad to see you are carrying your Bible young man." I responded, "Yes," as I opened my Bible to a randomly chosen scripture, in this case the book of Psalms. Looking up at him I sincerely asked, "Can you tell me what does, Psalm 91:4 say?"

Mom's jaw dropped as she grabbed my shoulder and blurted out sharply, "What are you doing?" I responded, "Well, he's memorized the whole Bible. I want him to say Psalm 91:4."

She apologized to the minister who was staring daggers at me, as he tried distractedly to change the subject while rapidly pumping the hand of the next person in line. Mom rushed me out the door with a painful grip on my hand.

He never did recite Psalm 91:4 for me!

****

I was abruptly returned to the present moment by the sound of the evangelist's fist slamming down for the umpteenth time on what had to be a weakening pulpit. Realizing that all church services eventually end, but fearing this one would be the exception, I was greatly relieved when the speaker stopped in mid-sentence, and announced the page number of the final hymn. I can only assume he felt the call of nature.

The march back to Fort Knox, and ultimately our beds, took less time than the lengthy revival meeting, but our arrival was at least an hour after lights out. Four AM seemed to come much earlier than usual the following morning.

After breakfast, our first smoke break, which for me and other non-smokers was just a break, was interrupted by our platoon leader who wanted to discuss the best course of action to dissuade Private Smith's propensity to tattle at will to the chaplain.

It was explained to Private Smith, who was strategically placed in the center of the gathering, that if he ever again reported any activity whatsoever to the chaplain, he would be drowned in an unflushed toilet. The ultimatum having been voiced eloquently by the platoon leader was assented to in a muffled grunt chorused by the entire platoon; a platoon that had been brought to the brink of mob mentality by the mandatory religious experience of the prior evening.

The tried and true military method of punishing the entire group for the infraction of one member achieved the desired result. The platoon felt the pressure, the platoon handled the problem, and everyone, including Private Smith, lived to enjoy another day of training.

****

NOTE: Psalm 91:4 reads, "He shall cover thee with his feathers, and under his wings shalt thou trust: his truth shall be thy shield and buckler."

Written by my childhood biblical hero David, and arbitrarily selected by my young fingers, Psalm 91 is an encouragement to anyone experiencing stressful times as well as soldiers heading to war.

Basic Training Graduation

CHAPTER FIFTEEN

With basic training and a short Christmas leave behind me, I headed for my next assignment at Fort Benjamin Harrison, Indiana in the dead of winter. All of my olive drab Army issue clothing was stuffed into my olive drab Army issue duffle bag, which rested in stark color contrast on the red and white back seat of my beautiful '61 Chevy Impala.

Beside me sat the love of my life, who, just happened to be due back for the beginning of second semester at Anderson College on the same day I was to report for duty. Fort Ben is located just thirty short miles southwest of Anderson. It was serendipity at its most serendipitous! Had I died and gone to heaven in central Indiana or what? It seemed so, but all good things have a limited life span, and so it was that my fondest dream and my future Mother-in-Law's worst nightmare were to last only three months.

Arriving at my new duty station that same afternoon I was impressed, and encouraged, by the classic structures and manicured lawns that made it look more like a nicely landscaped college campus than a military installation. I couldn't help thinking that I – had – arrived!

Classes at the U.S. Army Finance School began at 8 a.m. the following day, without the pressing urgency of the 4 a.m. start to which I had been accustomed. That, however, was the high point of the day. What I had expected to be a stimulating educational experience turned out to be an unbearably boring memorization of military manuals, directives and instructions written in military acronyms and decimal pocked reference numbers.

All classroom instruction was authoritatively dictated by

stone faced non-commissioned officers in a robotic fashion; probably the result of repeating the same material ad nauseam. When, on the rare occasion, an instructor did try to break with routine and lighten the mood by attempting to crack a joke, it was, more often than not, inappropriate for the coeducational class, and would have been likely to incur a sexual harassment based law suit a decade or so later.

Always aware and appreciative of every comparative blessing, I knew that my plight in this uninspiring class was a more desirable predicament than crawling in the mud, and experiencing the alternating discomfort of freezing and sweating, as was the lot of my Infantry brethren. I was never one to question a blessing.

In spite of the monotonous presentation, we did learn to accurately compute military pay vouchers, and became proficient at disbursing monies to deserving members of the military. Department of the Army civilians, who enjoyed a far better lifestyle, as well as a lot more money than their uniformed contemporaries, also benefited from our newly acquired skills.

The boredom was pleasantly punctuated each day at 5 p.m. with the end of class. Our time was our own until lights-out at 10 p.m. At first, having my car with me added to after class and weekend freedom. The disadvantage of being one of the very few class members with wheels soon became blatantly obvious and more than offset the benefits.

Everyone needed a ride to somewhere. The more aggressive freeloaders even asked to borrow my shiny red Chevy, "just for a while to get a few drinks." In lieu of allowing this potential catastrophe to occur, I would take them downtown. More often than not they would direct me to the sleazier parts of town. Unpaid chauffeuring became a recurring nightmare. Weekends that weren't spent driving to and from Anderson for my own purposes were consumed by taking "friends" downtown or to the airport or picking them up therefrom.

CHAPTER SIXTEEN

Time seemed to pass quickly at Fort Ben, largely due to the all too short weekends in Anderson. With only one week of Finance School remaining, my classmates and I welcomed the news that our training for the next two days would be conducted outside the classroom. The two day course was entitled ESCAPE, EVATION AND POW CONDUCT. The whispered consensus of class members was that anything would be better than sitting in class. The consensus was wrong!

As we filed into a large Quonset style structure with no furnishings other than a lectern and several long olive drab wooden benches, it became obvious that "outside the classroom" didn't actually mean "outside."

With the exception of a one hour break for chow, we sat painfully erect and alternately, painfully slouched, through one lecture after another. The subject of each lecture extolled the importance of avoiding capture by the enemy, escaping if we were captured, and evading recapture should the initial attempt at avoidance fail. The final instruction covered how to properly conduct ourselves as prisoners of war, should all previous attempts fail. The lecture on Prisoner of War conduct emphasized in frightening detail the vital importance of being successful at avoidance.

The lectures of day one were followed on day two by the Army's go to training method, "Learn to do by doing." At 4 am we were roused from slumber and issued helmets and M-14 rifles - each loaded with 20 rounds of blank ammunition. With the exception of the annoyingly early start, the day held the promise of an interesting, maybe even fun experience. Piling into the backs of two deuce-and-a-half trucks we were transported through the dark, cold dampness of the predawn fog to a dense pine forest several miles from base.

After twenty minutes in the butt fracturing truck bed an officer emerged from the woods signaling the trucks to halt. Ordering us off the trucks into a loose formation, he told us that enemy troops had been detected in the woods and our assignment was to find and capture the hostiles. Smiles crossed the faces of my classmates-turned-soldiers as we prepared for a morning of fun and war-games.

The officer disappeared into the cab of the lead truck as two NCOs came out of the dense foliage at the edge of the woods and jogged to our position on the road. The trucks lumbered off and disappeared along with the pavement into the fog shrouded, sylvan scenery.

As if reenacting a scene from a WWII movie, the ranking Sergeant raised his rifle over his helmet as he barked, "Alright men, follow me. Stay spread out, and keep your eyes open." I was standing closest to the Sergeant and noticed he was wearing ear plugs. They seemed out of place, but I've never been one to judge another's attire. Maybe he had an ear ache, I reasoned.

That he did not have an ear ache became painfully clear about a minute later, when we had penetrated fifty yards into the woods. M-80s exploded on either side of our ragged column, accompanied by automatic weapons fire that rendered our inexperienced platoon dysfunctional as well as deaf.

Several more M-80s detonated, as the black and red uniformed aggressors fell upon us from our right and left flanks, weapons blazing and shouting orders to lay down our weapons. Even though their verbal commands were muted by our impaired hearing, the gestures were easily understood.

Two classmates who had apparently paid attention to the previous day's instruction regarding the importance of an early escape attempted to do so. Their bid for freedom was met with brute force as they were tackled to the ground by four large captors, and roughed up to the point of bleeding. With arms and hands bound to their sides they were dragged to the front of the platoon. Tears streaming down the cheeks of the taller of the two told us that the "fun" part of the war games was over.

The optimistic part of my being wanted to assume that these violent actions would be the culmination of our hands-on training for the day, and we would return to the wooden benches to critique the session.

That optimistic assumption was terminated with a painful thud as a rifle butt struck my shoulder, accompanied by the snarled command, "Move Yankee bastard!" My thought was that our adversaries were taking this exercise way too seriously, but discretion prevailed and I silently moved forward with the disoriented column.

As we were herded into the courtyard of what appeared to be an old stone prison, two more M-80s exploded with a deafening boom, enhanced by the stone walls and causing even the most hardened of our group to cover their ears in anticipation of the next blast. Our captors laughed.

The simulated terror escalated inside the compound as the two failed escapees were tied to power poles in the center of the courtyard. One of the captors assumed the role of interrogator and asked them what unit they belonged to. As instructed in training, they recited their respective name, rank and serial number. Before they could complete their mantra, the interrogator touched an electric cattle prod to the leg of the nearest prisoner. He reacted to the shock with a loud cry as our collective disbelief turned to a cold sweat fear.

Why was this happening? This was Indiana, not some foreign country! These pretend captors were part of the U.S. Army! Had they gone mad?

We were pushed and prodded into the dank, cold concrete interior of the building, separated into individual cells and ordered to keep our eyes fixed on the floor. The cell doors remained open to enable the guards in the center hallway to watch our every move.

A scuffle outside the cell ended abruptly as a classmate, now fellow prisoner, was literally thrown into the cell with me and ordered into the front-leaning-rest position. The guard turned to me and snarled, "Think you're special you Yankee bastard? I said FRONT LEANING REST!"

The previous day's instruction echoed in my memory, "Obey all reasonable commands and do not antagonize your captors." I immediately dropped into the front leaning rest position and the guard stormed out of the cramped, musty cell with the admonition to remain silent and not move a muscle.

My cell mate, assuming we were alone, dropped to the floor to rest his arms and encouraged me to do the same. I didn't move. I didn't talk; just shook my head no.

In seconds the guard with the cattle prod stormed through the doorway and growled in a sadistic tone to my cell mate, "You weak Yankee scum! You should follow the example of your stronger friend here," as he jammed the cattle prod into his shoulder. Jerking away in pain my cell mate hit the wall and, with great effort, resumed the front leaning rest position.

The guard turned his attention to me, speaking in an unconvincingly civil tone, "Are you that strong Yankee or are you cheating too?" I answered, "No, Sir."

What to do? Code of Conduct prohibits conversation with a captor beyond stating your name, rank and serial number. That same code advises against antagonizing your captor. I was face down on the cell floor with a cattle prod inches from my left ear...What to do? For some strange reason, my thoughts turned to David, my childhood hero. I didn't recall him facing a like situation, but what would he have done? At the same time I remembered the old axiom, "Discretion is the better part of valor," and remained silent.

I braced for the anticipated pain, but the guard's civil behavior continued. "Why don't you and I go outside for a smoke Yankee?"

"I don't smoke, Sir."

Losing his short lived civility he snarled, "That's too bad Yankee, maybe you should!"

I braced once again for the expected jolt of electricity, but instead felt the pain as he ground his muddy combat boot into my left hand. I remained silent as he turned and left the cell with no further words exchanged.

We had endured another hour or so of similar harassment when, probably for the sake of realism, several M-80s exploded in the courtyard followed by rifle fire heralding our rescue by friendly forces and the end of our ordeal.

I assume that most of my classmates accepted the value and necessity of the realistic simulation to which we had been subjected that morning. In spite of the measured electric shocks, the blood and tears of my fellow soldiers who tried to escape and my bloody, mud covered fingers, none of us completely lost sight of the fact that we were participating in a training exercise. The pain inflicted by our faux captors was actual and memorable, and their acting skills would have qualified them for award nominations in the theatrical world. The debriefing that followed our field exercise began with a cursory apology and rationale for the intense experience.

When we returned to the bleak interior of the Quonset building and reclaimed our places on the drab wooden benches that we had painfully occupied for the previous day's lectures, the agenda for the afternoon was announced: The Geneva Conventions.

****

A valiant move on the part of some well-meaning statesman, the Geneva Conventions were an attempt to legislate ground rules for the humane treatment of prisoners-of-war as well as non-combatants.

A review of the provisions of those Conventions was followed by graphic descriptions of horrifying atrocities that have been committed by renegade military forces that do not subscribe to those rules. Renegade forces, were further defined as several enemies encountered in past wars, as well as, of more pressing interest, the Viet Cong and North Vietnamese Army. The lecture emphatically confirmed the importance of escape and evasion. If getting our attention was the goal of this day's training, the objective was met.

At no time during basic training do I recall discussing, during our free time evening hours, the training events of the day. This day was different. The severity of our training, coupled with the detailed accounts of the hideous tortures that could be in our futures grabbed our attention.

Beer, bravado and philosophy flowed freely that evening as the conversation centered around avoiding capture, as none of those present seemed inclined to discuss the alternative.

"If it's gonna happen, it's gonna happen," began our resident fatalist.

Unwilling to accept that line of thinking and rejecting surrender to an undetermined fate, one alcohol emboldened member proclaimed loudly,

"I'd fight them to the last bullet then kill them with my bare hands until they killed me!"

A politely quiet, "Yeh, my ass you would," was heard from a reasonably sober classmate.

Several variations on the same theme continued, but the statement that haunted my thoughts the rest of the night was from a usually quiet guy who voiced, in his unruffled manner, that he would never submit to capture or torture and would, "Fight to the end, but save the last bullet for myself."

Maybe it was his unemotional manner of speaking that made his pronouncement seem more credible than the others. That he calmly considered suicide a viable alternative to humiliation, torture and a painful death, caused me to ignore the continuing alcohol enhanced drivel proffered by the rest of the group.

Mulling over the words of my quiet classmate evoked the memory of a tragic occurrence just five months earlier during basic training…

****

A long day at the rifle range had ended and I was sitting in the grass beside FOXTROT Company barracks engaged in my daily letter writing routine. An audible but muffled pop interrupted my ritual as did a shower of glass shards erupting from what had been a second story window. Wide eyed trainees exiting the building, reported that one of our members had ended his life. Military Police investigators pieced together the events leading to, but not the reason for, the suicide. It happened this way...

At the end of each day's practice at the rifle range, a member of the training cadre performs a visual inspection of each M-14 rifle fired that day. Each trainee passes before the inspector, presents his rifle and repeats the catchphrase, "No brass or ammo, Sergeant," attesting to the fact that he has no live or spent cartridges on his person or in his rifle. On this day our fellow trainee had lied.

Upon returning to the barracks we routinely cleaned and oiled our rifles. Instead of taking part in this maintenance ritual, the distraught trainee retrieved the purloined cartridge from his pocket and loaded it into the chamber of his rifle. Placing the barrel beneath his chin he performed the last act of his life. The bullet passed through his brain before disintegrating the barracks window.

I didn't know the boy. He was in First Platoon while I was a member of Fifth Platoon and even though we trained together every day for eight weeks, it is not surprising that our paths never crossed, as our Company strength totaled 250 men. His fellow platoon members were closest to the traumatic event and their reactions ranged from stunned silence to vomiting. The response of those in my platoon, as could be expected, vacillated between detached concern and morbid curiosity. At the very least I felt that the deceased soldier deserved a moment of quiet reflection.

My own silent mental review of the event focused on the question, why? Perhaps a "Dear John" letter from a girl at home that he felt was his future. Was he bullied in school and considered the harassment of the training cadre a continuation of the pain? Was he simply not mentally prepared to be a soldier? My silent query went on for some time without resolution. I eventually concluded that only God knew what mental torture preceded the bullet that ended our fellow soldier's pain. I returned to my letter writing without mention of the incident. I never shared bad news with the folks at home.

****

My reverie ended with the increased volume of conversation that seems to accompany excessive consumption of alcohol based beverages. Nervous laughter ensued as we all took solace in the realization that, as members of the Finance Corps, we had a better than even chance of avoiding a combat situation that would end in capture. With that unsubstantiated assurance we all returned to the barracks and slept the sleep of the exhausted.

****

Graduation from U.S. Army Finance School wasn't accompanied with the degree of excitement of graduating from high school, but we were all glad to have the experience behind us. My stress level was higher than that of my classmates as we would soon receive our new assignments and I did not want to leave this heaven-on-earth just thirty miles from my focus, my future, my love.

Unfortunately, graduation provided one last opportunity for the more callous members of the training cadre to get one more laugh at our expense. Two days prior to receipt of our orders listing our permanent assignments, we gathered into our respective classrooms, ostensibly, to "pick our assignments."

From a list that included several prime vacation destinations around the globe, we were to pick our next work station. The dream list of available positions included two openings in Honolulu, three in London, two in Paris and a host of others. The last two available assignments at the bottom of the page caught my undivided attention.

My heart jumped as I read, FT. BENJAMIN HARRISON, INDIANA. No one would want to stay in Indiana, except me, who was content to fulfill my military obligation within driving distance of the love of my life.

We were issued our orders the next day. The first thing I noticed, as my heart sank, was that they had been typed and dated the previous week. Mine read: Assigned to Finance and Accounts Office, Paris, France! In keeping with the training cadre's twisted sense of humor, the classmates who chose Paris and Honolulu were assigned to Ft. Benjamin Harrison, Indiana!

CHAPTER SEVENTEEN

After six hours over the Atlantic, our Military Air Transport Service flight touched down at Orly Airport on the southern edge of Paris, France. Not being a fan of flying, I was glad to be back on Mother Earth, even if it weren't on my chosen continent.

I was traveling with a classmate who had also requested Ft. Ben Harrison as his first choice during our "pick your assignment" travesty. With $23.00 between us, we deplaned and proceeded directly to the airport's currency exchange window to convert our meager cash holdings into an equally modest quantity of French Francs. I contributed $17.00 to our pool of funds while he added $6.00. That level of individual contributions seemed to establish a paradigm for most of our subsequent joint monetary dealings.

Our orders were to take a taxi from the airport to a government subsidized hotel, Le Studio Etoile, located near the Finance Office in downtown Paris. As both of us were from small towns we had never ridden in a cab let alone hired one. No problem. I had seen Cary Grant hail a cab in a movie once and felt confident enough to try.

I was relieved to find several cabs awaiting exiting travelers immediately outside the concourse of the airport. In my best Cary Grant imitation I smiled and waved at the driver of the first cab. He moved forward a car length and hopped out. Given our military attire he must have felt safe in assuming our nationality and attempted, in his best English, a phrase he had obviously committed to memory, "Where may I take you?"

In a failed attempt to read the name of our hotel printed on our orders, I answered, "Lee Studio EE-TOY-LEE." With a confused look on his face he reached for the paper in my hand.

His face brightened as he announced, "Ah oui, Le Studio ET-WAW!"

Motioning toward the cab with a courteous half-bow he continued, "Please monsieurs, get in." As my friend and I entered the cab I made a mental note to learn the language of my host country.

Arriving at our destination after a twenty minute ride, I asked the amount of the fare as we exited the cab. Reverting to his native tongue he responded with what sounded like, "Saunt fraun." I shrugged questioningly and extended my open palm with our entire wad of French currency. He took it from my hand and counted out ten of the ten franc bills. Jamming them in his pocket he returned the remaining fifteen francs to me with a smile and sincere sounding, "Merci monsieurs, au revoir," as he drove away.

With duffle bags in hand, we walked through the entrance of the hotel, a weather beaten door with peeling paint, to be greeted by a fellow American on his way out. A short conversation, consisting of our questions and his answers, ensued. When we had absorbed all of the information we thought we needed he asked us two questions.

"How did you get here?"

We replied, "A cab."

"And how much did you pay?"

Sensing what was coming I hesitated and then responded in a decibel level just above a whisper,

"One hundred francs."

He chuckled then confirmed our suspicion that we had been over charged…by five times the going rate!

****

With eighteen hours to kill until we could report for duty and receive our first meal on foreign soil, a gnawing hunger begged our attention. With fifteen francs between us, our options were severely limited, so we set out to find an inexpensive restaurant in downtown Paris.

As we walked the streets of the city we found that affordable eating establishments were rarer than friendly smiles. After one glimpse of us, our fellow pedestrians averted their eyes as they walked by. At first I assumed their behavior was simply big city snobbishness, but sadly realized that our uniforms seemed to be a turn-off to every Parisian we passed, with the exception of a few prostitutes and cab drivers who make their livings being cordial. Searching block after block, it became increasingly obvious that there was not, never was nor ever will be an inexpensive restaurant in downtown Paris.

During our futile search for sustenance we came upon a small bakery, easily identified by the goods displayed in the shop window. The large sign reading PATISSERIE meant nothing to us. Again, I really needed to learn the language.

Once inside, the homey essence of baked goods overwhelmed our senses as our eyes began feasting on the golden brown crusts of countless baked offerings. A flour dusted young lady behind the counter interrupted our euphoric state with a polite, but questioning, "Monsieurs?"

I smiled knowingly as I held up my index finger requesting, in my best attempt at international sign language, a moment to decide. As our focus turned to the price tags spiked into each item, the reality of our limited funding hit home.

My roommate zeroed his attention on a six inch round cake-like creation with what he identified as a small peach-half resting on top. There were two of them priced at seven and a half francs each. As recent graduates of the U.S. Army Finance School, we calculated that our fifteen remaining francs would cover the cost. Carefully transporting our take-out dinners back to our sparsely furnished hotel room we prepared to feast.

With no eating utensils we began to break off and bite into small portions of our respective cakes, finding the bland taste to be reminiscent of a large communion wafer, albeit a puffy one. It didn't matter, we were starved. Saving the peach-half for dessert, I commented on its small dry appearance. We surmised that maybe peaches grow smaller in France, given the probability that they were raised in the same mineral depleted soil that had been reused annually since before the dark ages.

We found that our luck hadn't changed as the "peach-half" was actually a rapidly drying raw egg yolk! I never did find out what that baked concoction was called, but it didn't matter as I had no intention of ever ordering another.

****

Upon reporting for duty the following morning, we were guided to the cafeteria on the basement level of the three story finance building. Never had breakfast tasted so good.

Before the wolfed-down meal had reached our eager stomachs, we were rushed to the second floor for an interview with the Officer-In-Charge of the Class B Finance Agency at Camp des Loges.

Polished brass on his starched uniform gave us the impression that we were about to be interviewed by a straight laced military figure, but his soft spoken, pleasant manner exuded more civilian attributes than military. Although I was expecting to work at the main finance office in downtown Paris I was not disappointed when, at the conclusion of the interview, he offered me the position at Camp des Loges. Being offered an assignment rather than being ordered was a new experience in my short military career. My decision that I wanted this guy for my next boss was made early in the interview.

Further influencing my decision was the previous evening's experience in the dank, fixture-poor hotel room. We were informed that our accommodations of the previous night would be our quarters for the duration of this assignment. The hotel's plumbing included a single pull-chain toilet, located in the hallway of the second level to be shared by the occupants of four other nearby rooms. The amenities within the room were limited to two lumpy beds of questionable history, a sink and a bidet, the latter of which I had to explain to my roommate, was not a horizontal urinal as he had originally assumed.

****

Camp des Loges was headquarters of USERCOM (United States European Command) and was the work-a-day world of fourteen General Grade Officers, three of whom were French. SHAPE (Supreme Headquarters of Allied Powers in Europe) and NATO (North Atlantic Treaty Organization) were only a few miles from Camp des Loges, and rounded out the impressive stomping grounds of one of the largest concentrations of high ranking military personnel in the world. To my pleasant surprise I soon found that where there are generals there are also amenities.

Riding in the back seat of an Army sedan through the heavily guarded gates of Camp des Loges, my first impression was that I might have been assigned to a resort. The grounds and buildings were immaculate, and all visible personnel were attired in Class A uniforms.

The driver dropped me in the front of a dorm-like building that would be my home for the remainder of this tour. I stowed my duffle bag in a corner of the nicely appointed room and proceeded to the mess hall. To refer to this upscale dining facility as a mess hall was a gross misuse of terms, but this is the Army. China plates replaced the trays common to other military mess halls.

Bothered by the words, "mess hall", which seemed out of place, I decided to look it up. It seems that the original Latin word morphed into a French word that degenerated into an English word. I concluded that words, much like people, do not always look like their antecedents.

To the good fortune of all residents of Camp des Loges, an over achieving Army cook, who had risen to the much deserved status of Chef, directed his hand-picked staff of kitchen assistants in the daily creation of haute cuisine. Presentation of the daily fare alone would have qualified this chef and crew for employment at most five star restaurants. I was soon to realize the good stuff associated with my new assignment didn't stop with comfortable quarters and good food.

During the previous day's interview, the young officer had asked what motivated me to enlist in the Finance Corp. I explained that I intended to further my education using the GI bill during, or after, completing my military obligation. He was a Harvard graduate and sincerely valued education. Before I had completed the second week under his command, he had cut the governmental red tape and paved the way for my enrollment at the University of Maryland, European Division. The university's extension campus was located in a suburb of Paris.

It was an all work, no frills educational experience, but I had no complaints as my plan was unfolding faster than I had imagined. It got even better when I discovered that my out-of-pocket expense was limited to twelve dollars per course.

A precise forty hour workweek at the office allowed sufficient time at the end of each workday to grab chow before catching the Paris bound bus to my 6 pm class. Classes ended at 10 pm just in time for the return bus to camp. All courses were conducted by qualified professors, who had been fortunate enough to draw a teaching assignment in the Paris environs. The academic requirements and study regimen were the same as on any stateside campus, albeit without the extracurricular activities, or the parties or the protests.

Being blessed with a Class A pass – the military equivalent of a Carte Blanche for off-duty hours – meant that my free time was my own. I could go anywhere in France, and engage in any legal activity, between 5 pm on Friday and 8 am on Monday. Weekends allowed ample time for study, and on occasion, absorbing as much European culture as my limited interest in that pursuit would allow. I visited many of the obligatory museums, monuments, icons, landmarks and events in Paris and surrounding cities and towns.

One event that piqued my interest was the Twenty-four Hours at LeMans, the world's oldest sports car endurance race. The USO had organized a no-frills bus trip to the famous event for a ticket price of $14.00. The reasonably priced tickets assured us a seat on the bus, but not at the track. Upon arrival at the track, we found that our "seats" consisted of a piece of earth on the safe side of the fence about 200 yards from the grand stand.

For six hours my fellow attendees and I stood, leaned and reclined near the fence, observing the occasional car racing by, until the improbable combination of inactivity and physical exhaustion forced us to hike back to the bus. An unsuccessful attempt at sleeping upright in the school bus style seats rounded off our day.

Had I been an impassioned racing enthusiast the whole ordeal could have been enjoyable, but from my perspective the race was not only a test of endurance for the cars and drivers, but for the spectators as well. Twenty-four unbroken hours is too long for any party.

****

Viewing the Mona Lisa or Venus de Milo in the protected environs of the Louvre Museum is a special experience, but meeting a living icon up close and personal, not to mention unexpectedly, makes a memorable and treasured moment.

Thus it was that three weeks after the Le Mans experience, my roommate and I found ourselves perusing an extensive display of antique, as well as state of the art jet aircraft at the Le Bourget Airshow. Wandering aimlessly without an agenda or particular direction in mind I commented to my friend that we were pretty much alone. The crowd was slim. Maybe we were early, or the air show was already closed; our usual run of luck would evoke such concerns.

My study of the French language was progressing, but not to the point of being able to accurately interpret the subtleties of the more detailed signage. No worries, I didn't like crowds anyway and no one was asking us to leave.

Rounding one of the displays I noticed a sign printed in Russian, French and English announcing that on display directly in front of us was the actual Vostok space capsule that had carried a Russian Cosmonaut on the first manned space flight to orbit the Earth.

To my pleasant surprise, a short statured man with an athletic build and a constant smile sat next to the display in a nondescript folding chair. The man was Yuri Gagarin - the first man in space. He stood up as we approached and extended his hand. I shook his hand and uttered a sincere, "Pleased to meet you." He nodded as a taller man in a business suit came forward and asked if we would like one of the booklets entitled VOSTOK 1. Several copies were displayed on a folding table in front of us. He did all the talking while Yuri remained silent.

Thanking him, I started leafing through the booklet and found a picture of Yuri in his space helmet. I asked if I could have his autograph and the man said enthusiastically, "Of course, of course!" He handed the booklet and his pen to the cosmonaut who smiled broadly while inscribing his signature under the picture.

My friend had moved on to the next display, apparently not realizing the import of the moment, or maybe in fear of being observed consorting with Russians. Whatever his reasoning, he missed the opportunity to view the inside of the capsule. As I gazed at the cramped, instrument crammed cockpit it was obvious that anyone, even an inch taller than Colonel Gagarin, would not have fit in the capsule. More visitors were coming so, with another round of hand shaking, I bid them goodbye.

Yuri Gagarin

****

In March 1968, a jet trainer crashed in Kirzhach, Russia. The pilot, Colonel Yuri Gagarin, and his student pilot were killed. Whether the cause was accidental or otherwise, became the subject of much speculation immediately afterwards. The revered cosmonaut had been outspoken regarding the death of a friend and fellow cosmonaut in an earlier crash of an experimental space craft. His contention was that the accident should not have happened, and was the direct result of inept handling of the space program by Russian officials who expedited the launch schedule without sufficient testing. The spacecraft, and the cosmonaut, burned upon reentry.

The cause of the crash that killed Colonel Gagarin remains undetermined. The results of several unsanctioned investigations of events preceding the tragedy resulted in the unofficial consensus that voicing open criticism of government officials, in a totalitarian state, is far more risky than volunteering for an untested space flight.

On the personal level, my chance meeting with Yuri Gagarin lasted less than fifteen minutes, but I feel privileged to have experienced his broad smile and warm handshake.

****

That evening, mulling over my fortuitous encounter with the world famous cosmonaut, my thoughts turned to another first-in-space moment that occurred in 1962 when Colonel John Glenn became the first American to orbit the Earth. I never met John Glenn face to face, but found out shortly after his famous flight that he and I shared a similar appreciation, though separated by a period of eleven years, for the same geographical location on the planet...Muskrat Bottom!

In 1941, three years before my birth, John Glenn took his first flying lessons at Harry Clever Field in New Philadelphia. The first of his many training flights took off from the west end of the single runway located less than sixty yards from the east end of Muskrat Bottom, my childhood playground. I try to imagine the thrill he probably felt as he soared over the bottom land, and how it may have compared with his first flight into space twenty-one years later.

As a child my imagination soared as I roamed the warm loamy surface of that same spot of Earth pursuing one adventure after another. My childlike flights of fantasy were far less noteworthy than Colonel Glenn's flights, but no less thrilling.

CHAPTER EIGHTEEN

It was mid-October 1965, and I had completed one full year of active duty. My immediate boss, a young Sergeant we called Mac, asked me if I would like to celebrate the occasion by spending the weekend with his young family. It had rained most of the day, but the weekend promised to be beautiful. I accepted his kind offer, and grabbed a change of clothes as soon as the work day ended. He was four years my senior, and on the first year of his reenlistment. His family, a three-year-old girl, two-year-old boy and his pregnant wife had accompanied him to his present assignment.

It was almost twilight as we arrived at their tiny bungalow. It was located just outside of Paris, adjacent to a ferry landing on the left bank of the Seine River. A much used train track delineated the rear limits of their small lot, just thirty feet from the back door. The rumble of passing trains, which occurred about every four hours around the clock, interrupted my sleep later that night, but seemed to have little effect on the children's sleeping schedule.

Mac's pretty wife had gone to great lengths to prepare a perfect dinner. I offered to help by keeping their kids entertained while she put the finishing touches on the meal. We had just sat down at the small table when a frantic knock on the front door interrupted our dinner.

Mac opened the door to see a very damp mademoiselle in tears. Mac's command of the French language was nil, and my progress in learning the language hadn't prepared me to interpret her sobbing plea for help. With a combination of gestures, sign language and tearful French, our uninvited guest explained that she had missed the last ferry across the river.

Mac's offer to drive her to her home, via the nearest bridge, was met with a panicked refusal. She pointed to several rowboats tethered to a rickety looking dock less than fifteen yards from the house. My host was a sucker for a sad story, and I could see by his sympathetic countenance that he was going to solve her problem. He reasoned that it couldn't take more than fifteen minutes to row her to the ferry landing on the opposite side of the river.

With Mac's small family waving from the front door, we boarded the only rowboat that had oars. As I held the craft still, Mac helped our passenger get in. It seemed like a good time to ask if he knew who the boat belonged to, if we should ask permission to use it and, most pressing on my mind, did he know how to row a boat?

Ignoring the first two concerns, he answered, "How hard could it be?"

My confidence in our chance of success took another hit as I sat down and noticed how really wide the river looked from surface level! Mac's brave response echoed in my thoughts as he fumbled to get the first oar in its lock. After retrieving it the second time from the water, he succeeded. The other oar was less challenging. I pushed us away from the dock as he awkwardly coaxed our small craft in the direction of the opposite bank.

It was probably bad timing, but again I asked, "Shouldn't we have asked permission to use the boat?"

Straining at the oars to keep the boat on course against the current, he grunted through clenched teeth, "We're bringing the damn thing right back!"

As we reached the mid-point in our crossing, the current seemed to take on a life of its own and we began drifting down stream. Sensing that he was not the only force controlling the boat, Mac panicked, and tried to correct our course by alternating his pull on the oars which sent us into a slow spin. It reminded me of the Tilt-A-Whirl ride at the Tuscarawas County Fair which I didn't care for either.

I shouted for him to stop rowing until we were pointed in the right direction, as our terrified passenger slid from her seat onto her knees, and began imploring God to do something! Her frantic petition to God, "Mon Dieu, Mon Dieu," was easy enough to interpret, as I was about to consider prayer myself!

Mac regained his composure, resumed a synchronized pull on the oars, and through some quirk of fate or Divine intervention, we regained our original heading. It was comparatively smooth sailing as we neared the opposite bank. "Bank" was the operative word, as there was no flat shoreline visible in either direction. Our original destination, the ferry landing, was nowhere in sight! He stopped rowing and we floated gently along the river's edge, allowing me to grab a low hanging branch and bring our boat to a stop. Using the branch I pulled us the last few feet to the bank. Mademoiselle, still on her knees, thanked God in very emotional French and stood in preparation to get out.

Mac, obviously feeling somewhat the accomplished seaman, took on the demeanor of a ship's Captain and began bellowing instructions to his First Mate, "Hold 'er steady!"

Assuming he was referring to the boat rather than our passenger, I locked my boots under and around my seat and held on to the branch with both hands. Although not as strong as in the center of the river, the current still presented a challenge to my contorted attempt to, "Hold 'er steady."

The bank shot up about eight feet at an acute angle from the water's edge making a formidable obstacle to overcome, but we were determined to offload our passenger and get back across the river before complete darkness became another obstacle. While Mac pawed at the bank with an oar, Mademoiselle stumbled to the bow of the boat. Mac climbed out onto the muddy base of the bank, grabbed a protruding root, and extended his hand to the girl.

Fear returned to her face as she considered the steep bank. Using basic hand motions, he showed her how to grab exposed roots to get up the steep incline to level ground. As she got a foothold in the soft dirt and grabbed onto the nearest root, Mac put both hands on her derriere and pushed with great effort. The girl crested the top with a gasp of relief. Or maybe from having her butt grabbed! Regardless, regaining her composure she turned toward us, waived her mud covered hand, and repeated several times a sincere, "Merci, Merci," and headed in the direction of the now distant ferry landing

The satisfaction of completing a successful mission of mercy and the knightly feeling of having helped a damsel in distress lasted until we turned our attention to re-crossing the river, which from this side, looked even wider! What we first thought to be an optical illusion was not. From our current vantage point Mac's house could not be seen and the river actually had broadened. During the original crossing we had drifted more than a quarter of a mile downstream!

I offered to row us back across as Mac looked exhausted and I felt confident that I could do a better job having had the benefit of watching my young Sergeant do it wrong.

He asked hopefully, "Do you think you can?"

I savored the moment, as I parroted his earlier words, "How hard can it be?"

We pushed off from the muddy bank and I began pulling on the oars.

It was good to feel the boat responding to my effort, as it moved in the direction I intended. It had been a long time since I last rowed a boat and it was exhilarating. It was going well until we gained the middle of the river and, as before, the boat yielded to the increased current and headed down river.

The thought of losing control of my craft equidistant from either shore sobered any smugness I had felt regarding my ability to row a boat. A fleeting moment of panic ensued until I realized that we were still headed in our intended direction, albeit indirectly. I pulled as hard as physically possible as darkness closed in making seeing difficult. Encouragement came, and panic subsided, as I glanced over my shoulder at the tree lined shore silhouetted against the last vestiges of daylight. We were almost there! I continued paddling with enough force to run the boat aground and we stepped off onto damp, solid ground.

While catching our breath, I asked what the plan might

be for returning the boat. We couldn't carry it, nor could we pull it along the vegetation tangled bank, and pure exhaustion dictated that we would not be paddling back upstream! Hoping the owner wouldn't need his boat anytime soon we agreed to return it first thing in the morning. Securing the boat to the nearest tree, we began our hike back to the house, which to our surprise, was almost a mile from where we stood!

Our lovely dinner was cold, but not as cold as our reception from Mrs. Mac. Luckily, somewhere in the night, Mac regained the favor of his lovely bride of four years, and after a quick, hot breakfast at 6:00am, we headed for our landing site to retrieve the boat.

It was gone!

As we walked back home, Mac's only comment was, "What kind of a creep would steal an old boat?"

CHAPTER NINETEEN

Of all my faults, the one that has caused me the most stress, time and money is undoubtedly, the inability to say "NO" when I know, for my own good, I should.

It was Friday evening of the week following my eventful weekend at Sergeant Mac's house, and I had just propped up in my bunk, trying to find a comfortable position to spend an hour or so studying for an upcoming test.

A single loud wrap on the door interrupted my concentration. It was obviously a rhetorical rap as the door swung open before I could respond with a, "Come in," or "Who is it?" or "Go away." I beheld a vaguely familiar face, but didn't make a positive ID until I heard his southern twang as he asked, "Wot's up?"

His greeting alerted me to the uncomfortable probability that something actually WAS "up," and I was simply unaware of my part in the proceedings.

Telling the truth seemed the most reasonable response, so I answered, "I'm studying for a test."

He countered with, "That don't sound like no fun to me. Thar's a carnival set up rat outside camp. Wah don't let's go?"

We were barely acquaintances, let alone friends. Our paths seldom crossed as he was assigned to a Motor Pool company on the opposite side of camp.

I knew his nickname was Sponge, which I had originally assumed was a derivative of his last name that was something akin to Spongarelli or Spongaretti or Spongiello. I later learned the moniker had been bestowed by past acquaintances that had fallen prey to his tendency of borrowing money from them with no thought or plan of repayment.

Again I whined, "Uh, I really have to study."

He whined in response, "C'mon man, y'all cin study tomorra. This is the only tam ah cin go, and sides it ain't no fun by m'self."

Reading between the lines, I assumed that Sponge was again financially embarrassed and looking for assistance. However, I knew from past experience that offering to pay his way to the carnival, just to get him off my back, would set a precedent for future borrowing.

He just stood there staring at the floor, in uncomfortable silence, obviously waiting for a more favorable response to his invitation. As with any competent con man he could read in my involuntary facial expression that I was weakening. His tone shifted seamlessly from nagging to gentle pleading, complete with a puppy dog eyes expression. I finally realized that Sponge was more than a fund-less con man, he was genuinely lonely as well.

"Oh, what the hell," I thought. It was just a ten minute ride around the perimeter of the camp and only two hours out of my total weekend. Besides, maybe I could instill some financial values and responsibility into this budding reprobate. The warm feeling that sometimes accompanies a wave of 'do-gooderism' swept over me as I considered the mission that lay before me, along with the memory of my part in the previous week's rescue of the damsel-in-distress at the Seine River ferry landing.

With no further delay I announced that I would go with him, with the proviso that our return would be no later than 8:00 pm. He happily agreed to the condition and we headed for the bus stop.

As we boarded the bus he asked, "Bah the way, cin y'all lend me a fav till payday?" I smiled as I handed him the French franc equivalent of five dollars.

****

Amusement parks, circuses and the like are not included on my go-to list of entertainment options. Accordingly, eight o'clock couldn't come soon enough as I endured, with some effort, what the carnival had to offer. The event seemed to be sponsored, and largely attended by, Gypsies of no particular national origin. With the Beaujolais priced at twenty centimes per small bottle, it was no wonder that most attendees were in various states of inebriation. A few rides, occupied mostly by children, were powered by small noisy engines that spewed visible exhaust fumes into a stagnant atmosphere already laden with the acrid smoke of French cigarettes protruding from the corners of old men's mouths. As they carried on various conversations, in multiple European dialects, the stubby cigarettes stuck to their lower lips and wobbled up and down like a smoldering polygraph needle.

Within ten minutes Sponge disappeared into the crowd, his need for camaraderie apparently having been satisfied. Looking around for something to occupy my time, I found one of many vendors and bought a bottle of Beaujolais. I never pretended to be a wine connoisseur, but I know lip-puckering bad when I taste it. I had heard that Beaujolais should be consumed while young. This stuff was ready for the vinegar barrel, but what should I have expected for five cents?

Eight o'clock came and went, as did the last bus back to camp! Why had I waited for him? Why had I agreed to come in the first place? Why did I feel sorry for people like him? And most pressing, why, as it worked its way through my digestive system, did I drink that disgusting bottle of wine?

I located Sponge thirty minutes later. His excuse for being late seemed plausible. He had met a Gypsy girl who had invited him to have dinner with her family in their trailer. I was only interested in getting back to camp, but tried to be civil by feigning interest and asking what he had eaten.

"Well, we didn't akchly eat, and ah only met her brother, but she was a grite kisser!"

"And what did this 'kissin'' cost you?"

"Nothin."

"Do you have any money left?"

Reaching in his pocket he snorted, "'course ah do!" But he

didn't.

"Damn, she done stoled mah twenty-fav dollars!"

"You only had five."

No, ah had twent…" Stopping in mid-sentence, his face flushed as he remembered the cash I gave him.

"Damn! Her brother must o' filched it outta ma pocket!"

"So, you had to take your pants off to kiss her? Never mind. Tell me later. We have a four mile walk in the dark…the last bus has gone!"

As we walked out onto the main road, I took some enjoyment in the irony of a budding con man being conned. Of course, the experience would probably only serve to sharpen his nefarious tendencies. Unfortunately ten seconds into our walk, Sponge came up with a better idea.

"Wait! The back gate to camp cain't be more 'en a couple hundert yards through them woods. We can be thar in tain minutes!"

"I don't think that's a good idea," I cautioned.

"C'mon man, it'll be quicker and 'sides thar's probly a gang of Algerians* waiting on the road to jump us!"

"How do you know there are no Algerians in the woods?"

"Don't be silly, man."

*Note: Many Algerians immigrated to Paris from French Algeria in the 1960s due to political unrest in their homeland. Most were good people, but as in all populations, there existed a small criminal faction.

That was the first sensible thing he had said. Who would be in the woods in the middle of the night? With only two hundred dubiously estimated yards, and near complete darkness between us and the back gate, we began our ill-conceived trek in the direction determined by our self-appointed guide. The carnival lights faded then disappeared completely as we penetrated the woods. Threatening rain clouds added one more level of challenge to our semi-blind stumbling, but with no better plan, we plodded on in the direction that Sponge assured me would lead to the back gate.

Luckily, I detected a hazy illumination above the tree tops to our far left. Metaphorically, as well as literally, clouds appear to have a silver lining when viewed against a bright solar backdrop. When viewed against a night time sky from the middle of a dark wood, they cast the hazy reflection of any man-made light beneath them. I shared this trivial piece of atmospheric phenomena with Sponge, and suggested that we change course toward the welcoming hue cast by the security lights of Camp des Loges. We had trudged more than the estimated two hundred yards already, and I guessed that the camp was still over half a mile away!

It was 11:30 when we reached the back gate, covered with painful bruises, cuts and punctures from countless encounters with thorns and sharp sticks. Our soaked socks were sloshing in boots filled with smelly water acquired while crossing an unexpected brackish water feature. To my surprise, the gate was locked and, as far as I could determine, unmanned.

My suggestion to follow the security fence around the perimeter of the camp to the front gate was met with abject refusal. As Sponge explained to me, in that twangy southern drawl that sometimes makes a bad idea sound like a pronouncement of down home, back country wisdom, it would be more expedient to avoid the nearly mile and a half walk. We could go ten feet vertically over the gate and be inside camp in less than five minutes. He hadn't been right yet, but I was simply tired of the struggle.

Promising myself that I would never again try to reform a born reprobate, I watched him negotiate the conveniently spaced hinges of the gate, and then drop to the other side with the ease of a Commando...or someone who, of necessity, had climbed a similar fence before! I followed suit, but hesitated at the top to consider how far down ten feet looked from up there. Then again, it really didn't matter, as I was willing to break any number of bones to bring this nightmare to a close.

The instant I hit the ground the entire area was flooded with blinding light, as two very deep, very loud voices bellowed in unison, "Halt!"

A mental blur ensued as I envisioned my future behind bars, and all because I attempted to befriend a lonely loser, only to wind up breaking into a government facility; and that, on the heels of rescuing a distressed damsel, facilitated by using a stolen boat! Was I headed for a life of unintentional crime or a career as a bumbling social worker?

When the dust settled, I was remanded into the custody of my Commanding Officer, who was called from a Friday night poker game to transfer me from MP Headquarters to my comfortable barracks.

I apologized profusely, but he simply said, "Just stay away from that SOB. By the way, your timing couldn't have been more perfect. I was losing my ass to the Colonel. Now I'll go rescue my wife from the Colonel's wife."

I loved that guy!

As for Sponge – he was put in the brig, as he had already been on restriction and violated his sentence by leaving post. I sincerely hope that he got his wayward tendencies under control. I never saw him or my five dollars again.

****

Being the quintessential homebody, I had no trouble staying in my room on most weekends, reading, studying and writing letters home. Besides, the assumption was that I would remain in this current assignment for the duration of my short military career. Another life lesson about to be learned: Don't bank on your assumptions…

Fourteen months into my tour of duty at Camp des Loges, my well-tuned plan was unexpectedly interrupted by the receipt of orders reassigning me to Fort Riley, Kansas. No hints, no warnings, just orders.

Mixed emotions consumed every conscious moment. I was excited at the prospect of an unscheduled fifteen day leave to be shared unequally between my future wife and my family and friends, before reporting to Fort Riley. On the other hand, I could not finish my current classes, nor would I receive credit as they would be considered incomplete.

Grumbling to my Commander about the glitch in my plan and my wasted effort, his unruffled response was, "No education is wasted if you remember and apply what you learn." It turns out that he was right.

Five days later I boarded a plane at Orly Airport with my orders, my duffle bag and my acrophobia, and soared to unnerving heights, the only comfort being the sounds of Simon and Garfunkel emanating from the ear buds provided by a caring stewardess.

CHAPTER TWENTY

A fifteen day leave to a soldier in love is like a drop of water to a thirsty man. Being an ocean apart from the girl of my constant thoughts and dreams for fourteen months, then barely touching base before leaving again was torment for both of us.

Romeo and Juliet may have felt that, "Parting is such sweet sorrow," but according to Shakespeare's telling of the story, they were intending to meet on the "morrow."

Unfortunately, I had a war to attend and no idea when our "morrow" would come…if ever.

With an overwhelmingly sick feeling in the pit of my stomach, I boarded a train in Dennison, Ohio bound for St. Louis and, ultimately, Fort Riley, Kansas. Although my orders directed me to Fort Riley, the consensus of all concerned was that the final destination would be Southeast Asia.

With no other visible military personnel on the train, I wrestled alone with a bout of self-pity, but to my surprise won the close match with a well-placed emotional slap in the face. Arriving at the St. Louis terminal with a renewed optimism, I had about an hour to kill before re-boarding, and my legs needed stretched. I wandered into a small store front that sold snacks, smokes and paper backs. I decided I needed something to occupy my mind, so I perused the book rack and selected two unmemorable titles.

As a non-smoker, I have no idea what prompted me to stop at the cigar counter. The fluctuating, maudlin state of my emotions may have fostered this out-of-character impulse. I got the clerk's attention and pointed to a cigar of unrecognized manufacture - at least to me.

As he retrieved my choice from the humidor, a well-dressed, attractive lady in or around her fifties, wearing a tasteful array of jewelry and a pleasant perfume, stepped up close to me and put her hand on my arm. She turned her attention to the clerk, instructing him to, "Give this young man the entire box."

I blurted out, "Mam, I don't..." She stopped me in mid-sentence.

"Shush, I insist. I just want you to know how much I appreciate you young men in the Service."

I started again, "But..." This time I was interrupted by a younger, even more attractive woman, bejeweled and perfumed almost to excess.

"Don't try to change her mind. This is my mother and she has a soft spot for soldiers."

The mother paid the clerk, telling him to keep the change. I thanked them profusely for their kindness and bid them goodbye. By then, I saw no reason to tell them I didn't smoke.

The daughter turned to me and said, "We both love soldiers. Good luck, Honey." Then planted an unsolicited kiss on my unsuspecting lips!

It was a Norman Rockwell moment, and I was too dazed to enjoy it!

****

At 2 am the following morning, the train pulled into a dark, unmanned depot in Junction City, Kansas. I grabbed my duffel bag and exited the train. My feet barely touched the pavement before the train pulled away and disappeared into the night.

I stood under a street light contemplating my next move. It wasn't an uncommon occurrence to get stranded during an individual transfer from one assignment to another. The lack of arrangements on the Army's part often necessitated improvisation on my part. Needing something to pass the time and calm my attitude toward the Army's inattention to detail, I decided to take up smoking; at least on a temporary basis. I rummaged through my duffel bag and located my box of gifted cigars and extracted one. After tearing off the plastic wrapper, I placed the sweet tasting thing in my mouth and held it in place with my teeth. At that point I realized I had nothing with which to light it, thus ending my first attempt at smoking.

My frustration ended as a car slowed to a stop in front of me. The driver stretched his head out of the window and asked if I needed a ride to Fort Riley.

Relieved and thankful I hopped in. I asked why he was out in the wee hours of the morning, and he explained that the small depot was on his way from downtown Junction City to his home near the base. He often picked up soldiers who were stranded at the closed depot.

The ride to Fort Riley was less than ten minutes, but in that time I listened to a synopsis of the driver's recent life history. Having a captive audience, he continued the one sided conversation, telling me that only one bar in the tiny city stayed open late and he spent each evening there with his friends, Jim Beam and Jack Daniels.

His attempt at humor went right over my head, until I identified the odor that permeated the interior of the car as the exhaled fumes of one or the other of his "friends."

He was apparently a skilled driver as well as an experienced drinker as he never veered from his lane, and deposited me safely at the front gate of the Army base. He refused payment for gas, but accepted a handful of cigars from my plentiful supply and said, with a slight quiver in his voice, "You be careful now son, and if they send you to that hell hole in 'Veet Nam', you keep your head down, ya hear?"

I was beginning to detect a pattern of concern with all the well-wishing from those with whom I had made only casual contact over the past thirty-six hours. Maybe their concern should have caused me concern, but I was beginning to experience an unexplained feeling of pride instead.

****

The "dog days" of summer took on new meaning in 1966

Kansas. Heat, humidity, boredom and a general disquiet concerning our immediate future attended every waking hour; a nasty combination of physical and mental irritants that made the three month stay seem to drag.

Ice cold beer, ingested daily in the heat of the late afternoon, provided temporary relief as well as something to look forward to earlier in the day. Our favorite watering hole in Junction City was known as Della's place. It was a clean, well-kept bar and short menu restaurant, owned and operated by a motherly sixty-year-old named...Della.

Della catered to military personnel looking for good food, drink and the ever present friendliness of her small staff. The bar surface was adorned with several gallon jars filled with edible delights including: Kosher dills, pork hocks, pickled pigs feet, eggs pickled in red beets, and assorted peppers in various degrees of hot. The only alcohol served was beer.

There were other bars in Junction City; some sleazy and some downright dangerous, but none had the downhome feel of Della's Place.

The tastes and smells of the home-canned offerings on the bar were not only delicious, but evoked pleasant memories of better times. Sensory stimulation is the fast track to recollection of past events. While enjoying an evening at this quaint bar/restaurant, I often thought of my grandfather and our Friday night gatherings in front of our black and white Philco television to watch the Friday Night Fights. Mom and Dad were heading for bed as Dad worked most Saturdays, and Grandma wasn't interested in pugilistic exhibitions. It was just Papaw and me.

Papaw was in charge of refreshments, and this ten year old was never disappointed in his presentation of the Friday evening fare. The unprinted menu changed from week to week. Alternately, we consumed pickled pigs feet or pork hocks or some other middle class delicacy. My favorite items were the more aromatic offerings including Limburger sandwiches with a thick slice of sweet onion, or sardines in oil with crackers. It was haute cuisine for the working class! There was no alcohol served by order of Mom!

CHAPTER TWENTY-ONE

Boredom was the natural by-product of living at Fort Riley awaiting our next assignment. I was content to read the day away, but that came with the risk of being tapped for some fairly undesirable "busy work", duties usually referred to by the unofficial military term, "Chicken Shit". Yard maintenance, garbage detail, painting, etc. are lumped under that designation.

"I need two men to act as guards for a prisoner transfer," a loud voice announced.

My concentration became intense as I gazed at the last word I had read so it would be obvious that I was much too engrossed in study to acknowledge the Sergeant's presumptive request. Silence fell over the barracks.

His highly polished combat boots squeaked as he approached my bunkmate and me. Pointing to each of us he said, "You're a man and you're a man, and let me see. Yes, there are two of you. Drop what your doin' and come with me."

Just because he said it was a "prisoner transfer" didn't necessarily mean it was going to be a prisoner transfer. The first thing you learn in basic training is if they ask for anyone who can drive a truck to step forward, those who step forward will be pushing a wheelbarrow for the rest of the day.

And if it were a prisoner transfer, what exactly was a prisoner transfer?

Within minutes the three of us were bouncing in an Army Jeep toward the Fort Riley Prison. Being unfamiliar with the layout of the fort, I couldn't say if the prison was located on the post or off, but it didn't really matter.

Daring to ask the inevitable question I inquired, "We're in

Finance, are you sure you got the right barracks?"

He responded, "You're both alive and warm, you'll do." Then he added with a chuckle, "We're shorthanded today, several of our guards shipped out yesterday for 'Nam. It's just like guard duty and you'll be back in time for chow."

It wasn't and we weren't!

The front gate opened and we drove through. Rolls of barbed wire topped off the eight foot high chain link fence that surrounded the entire compound. The Sergeant hopped out of the Jeep, and pointing, directed us to a small drab office building.

As he left us he said, "You'll get your assignment in there."

Inside we were greeted by a stone faced Sergeant who, without taking his eyes off of the register on his desk, said, "Name and serial number."

I assumed it was a question so I responded with the requested information, as did my fellow conscript.

Without lifting his head he instructed us to take one M-14 each from the arms rack, and one magazine each from the shelf beneath the rack. Each magazine was loaded with only three cartridges. I asked why.

Raising his head for the first time, with a smile bordering on a sneer, he said, "So you can defend yourselves if things get out of hand, and limit a prisoner's firepower to six rounds if he takes your weapons. Now, lock and load and report to building number two."

We got the impression that he didn't care for Finance personnel. We were often looked upon, incorrectly, as the spoiled kids on the block. The "grass is greener" syndrome plagues many folks.

As we left his office I thought I would try to be sociable, even if he wasn't and said, "Thank you, sir."

He responded, "Don't call me sir soldier. I'm not an officer. Call me Sergeant. I wear stripes and work for a living!"

Apparently his unwarranted envy extended to more than Finance personnel.

We proceeded to the cement block building with a large

2 on its windowless, unwelcoming door. Stepping inside, a guard sitting at a small olive drab desk instructed us to leave our weapons with him, as another guard explained that we were to take our assigned prisoner for a physical and psychological evaluation at the infirmary located on the opposite side of the compound. Then he added, in a hushed tone, that the prisoner was being held on a murder charge. He asked us to wait in the hallway while he and a third guard entered the cell and handcuffed the prisoner.

When they brought him out of the cell, I thought that we had been made the butt of a bad joke!

The prisoner appeared to be about thirteen with a thin, fragile looking build. We stood silent as the guard instructed us to take hold of him by his arms as they had. The guard at the desk returned our weapons which we slung on our shoulders to the far side of the prisoner. The inmate avoided eye contact with us and maintained the same eerie, distant smile he had when he was taken from his cell.

As we walked to the infirmary no words were exchanged between the three of us. A verbal exchange wasn't necessary, but the lack of conversation was awkward. I had never been in a like situation prior to this moment and felt very uncomfortable being in control of this fellow human being.

My mind searched for something to fill the silence other than the soft thud of our combat boots against the hot pavement. Should I ask where he's from? What unit he's with? Who had he killed, and why? All were inappropriate to the situation.

Casual conversation was impossible and certainly out of place, but soon became unnecessary as inmates on the second story confinement area broke the silence with taunts and epithets. At first I thought they were directed at our prisoner, but quickly realized that we, not he, were the intended recipients of the vitriolic barrage.

The most disturbing of the insults hurled at us mockingly called into question our bravery. The snarled question of one inmate asked why it took two big strong guys with guns to control a skinny little kid in handcuffs. The question was echoed by others from behind their barred windows. Oddly, I was wrestling with that same question, but from a different perspective. I was becoming more uneasy with my assignment. We continued walking while trying unsuccessfully to ignore the shouting.

Finally reaching our destination, we handed our prisoner over to the infirmary guard. The entire walk only covered the distance of a city block from our starting point, but seemed much farther.

During our three hour wait in the hot afternoon sun we struck up a conversation with an MP who happened by. We told him of our encounter with the shouting prisoners. He told us of an incident three days earlier in which an inmate had attempted to escape by scaling the perimeter fence, and was shot by a guard. The inmates had been in constant upheaval since. Apparently, protesting wasn't the exclusive prerogative of college students – anyone with a gripe was venting their opinion.

Our prisoner and his guard eventually appeared at the infirmary doorway. We began our silent walk back to his cell. There was no shouting this time; it was chow time and our tormentors were busy eating.

Leaving the prison compound that day, I had the same repulsive feeling that I might have experienced had I kicked a chained dog. Our young prisoner was actually older than he looked, and I'm sure his incarceration was justified, but I realized that afternoon that I was too empathetic toward human conditions for that type of duty.

A few months later in Vietnam, I would be faced with a situation where my empathy for those who look physically smaller and weaker could have been terminal.

****

By mid-August, thirteen of us had been formed into a small unit designated as the 28th Finance Detachment. Our orders were to report, as a unit, to Oakland Army Terminal for transport to an unspecified destination in Southeast Asia. Further orders would be received en route.

CHAPTER TWENTY-TWO

It was late August 1966 when our small unit boarded a regular commercial flight from Kansas City to San Francisco. Dressed in fatigue uniforms and laden with duffle bags and M-14 rifles, we attracted only moderate attention from the civilian passengers.

A few stared, others turned their heads in an attempt to ignore us, and some met us eye to eye with sad smiles that said without words, "We're sorry you have to do this." Together, they formed a nutshell representation of the diverse attitudes developing across the nation toward the burgeoning war.

The flight was unmemorable with the exception of the rapid ear-stabbing decent on to a runway of San Francisco International Airport, inviting concern from all onboard as to our pilot's landing skills.

Next to the tarmac an Army bus awaited our arrival, and immediately carried us to Oakland Army Terminal where we boarded the USNS General E.D. Patrick. The World War II vintage troop ship sailed the next morning with 2500 Soldiers and Marines aboard.

Until the moment the ship began an undetectable forward movement the sum total of my experience with watercraft had been as a passenger in a rowboat at the age of seven, a short ride on a pontoon when I was twelve and, most recently, the crossing of the Seine River incident ten months earlier. With those nautical encounters behind me I felt confident in refusing the Dramamine offered by a Navy corpsman as we sailed under the Golden Gate Bridge in the San Francisco Bay.

I remained silent as the corpsman asked repeatedly, "Do any of you get seasick?" I had heard somewhere that seasickness was all in the mind and besides this big ship was moving along smoothly, no rearing up and crashing down as I had seen on many editions of VICTORY AT SEA. In fact we were moving so slowly that I had to stare intently at the shore on either side just to confirm our forward progress. As the San Francisco Bay area slipped from sight behind us, the ship gained speed and within two hours we were on, what I perceived to be, the high seas.

USNS General E.D. Patrick sails under the Golden Gate Bridge

God was I sick! I beat a hasty retreat from the top deck to what Sailors and Marines call, "The Head." The incessant up and down of the ship and my nauseated reaction there-to, caused me to confine myself there-in.

The plumbing in this particular "Head" consisted of a row of ten porcelain toilets without seats that were affixed to a drain-pocked floor, with hand rail type piping on either side of each toilet. Were we actually to grasp and hold on to the piping while performing bodily functions suspended in mid-air?

It was an example of low maintenance nautical plumbing at its most expedient! The utility of the Spartan design exceeded the convenience, but functioned flawlessly.

There was no reprieve in this facility from the constant rolling motion of the ship. I continued to heave and hurl everything that was not attached to my internal anatomy, while the sloshing sea water contained in each toilet splashed over the edge with each vertical movement of the ship. The reason for the well-drained floor became evident as the sea water and other "stuff" flooded over my combat boots on its way to the nearest drain.

Crackers and peanuts comprised my strict diet for the next few days as nothing else would stay down.

****

On the second day out to sea the ranking officers on board, whose quarters by the way, were located in the center of the ship where movement is barely noticed, apparently became restless and decided that it would be entertaining to schedule an inspection of the troops. Most of my nearby shipmates were scurrying around in preparation for the Inspector General's appearance. I started preparing my bunk, known as a rack to Sailors and Marines, but soon gave up and laid my spinning head back on what passed for a pillow.

Inspector General is a functionary title rather than a designation of actual rank, and in this instance, was performed by a Lieutenant Colonel. My bunk mates implored me to stand up beside my bunk for inspection. God knows I tried! Failing the attempt, I sank slowly back on my bunk as the Inspector General entered the room.

"Ten-Hut" was the only thing I heard over the internal din pulsing in my ears. As the Inspector General neared our cubical the sergeant assisting him leaned over me and yelled, "Get up soldier!" I struggled to my feet and stood at a wobbly state of "Attention" as the Inspector General came to attention in front of me. Our eyes met and he immediately took a step back and in an unexpectedly soft voice said, "Lie down, son." He turned to the sergeant who had started toward me and said, "Its ok Sergeant."

Whether it was compassionate understanding or just fear of having his uniform defiled with bodily fluids, I was nevertheless grateful for his empathy.

Things seemed to get better over the next few days both internally and externally. The seas were calm and I was able to go up on deck and even began reading my paperbacks with no ill effects. In the normal course of a work day in the military, loafing around would have brought charges of malingering, but there were no assigned duties to avoid and the only enemy was boredom. Every day was the same; get up, eat peanuts, go top side to read and breath air, go back below deck, eat crackers, go to sleep, repeat.

A brief stop at Subic Bay on the island of Luzon, The Philippines, was the only break in our westward progress. It was an overnight stay. As the ship steamed out of the bay the next morning we officially entered the South China Sea.

CHAPTER TWENTY-THREE

We awoke the next morning to the sight of two Navy Destroyers, one on either side of our vessel. The presence of the well-armed ships could only mean that we had entered dangerous waters. We soon learned that a warship escort was standard operating procedure for troop transport ships in potentially hazardous seas. Most of us hadn't considered that we could be in peril this far from Vietnam, but along with this new concern came reassurance that we were being watched over by our own Navy. It was an emotional boost to see something besides endless miles of salt water and sky.

That moment was short lived as a real and more present threat appeared on the western horizon. The darkening skies announced the approach of what was to become a violent storm that would accompany us for the next forty-eight hours.

The decks were cleared of all personnel as the ship sailed under the black clouds. The rise and fall of the ship's bow reached exceptional heights and depths. During the worst of the storm we did not actually see the decks awash with each plunge of the bow as we were confined below deck. But there was no doubt about the extreme degree of vertical movement as our quarters were located in the bow of the ship and we were elevated and plunged with each wave as the ship plowed ahead. It was like being on a radically designed roller coaster at an amusement park except that it was not fun and we couldn't get off.

After two days of atmospheric bombardment, the sea calmed as did my stomach and we were permitted to go topside to enjoy the sun and breathe air. What an awesome sight it must have been the previous night, as the entire bow plunged beneath the water's surface then returned to a height of thirty feet above water level. It didn't take a degree in nautical engineering to figure that, in the worst of the storm on the previous day, our living quarters had been beneath the surface most of the time!

****

The next few days were smooth sailing which at first seemed like a good thing. With nothing to do other than sit on the deck and be lulled by the gentle sea, the lack of purposeful activity created a state of agitated boredom. Our immediate future seemed vague and worrisome at best, but after twenty-one days of being confined on or below deck we were more than ready for a change of venue – even if it was Vietnam.

Then, just when the morale and general mood of the troops had degenerated to the point of lethargy, relief came – we saw land!

As the coast of South Vietnam became more defined on the horizon, rampant speculation, hopeful rumors and official sounding hearsay circulated among the newer troops - those who were being deployed immediately after graduating from Advanced Infantry Training.

It is probably in the interest of security that the general policy of leaders in the military is to remain tight-lipped regarding impending movements and actions. However, that procedure unintentionally sets the stage for supposition and wild-assed guessing among the rank and file.

Those of us who had been in the service long enough to gain military street-smarts, knew that information is disseminated only on a "need to know" basis. We just assumed that we really didn't "need to know" and waited with acquired patience for whatever direction we would soon enough receive.

CHAPTER TWENTY-FOUR

By late afternoon, that same day, the USNS Patrick steamed slowly into the deep water bay at Cam Rahn, South Vietnam and came to a stop or more appropriately, "dropped anchor" several hundred yards off shore.

The rumor mill went immediately into high gear as to who would be disembarking on any of several "Mike" boats that were dieseling toward our ship. (Mike boats are diesel powered, waterborne transport vessels also known as Landing Craft.) The rumors were variously confirmed or denied as the large contingent of Marines began forming on deck for debarkation.

As the Mike boats came alongside, the Marines began boarding the transports single file; some used rope ladders while others descended narrow ladder type staircases to the large, open hulls of the landing crafts. The process took several hours – there were a lot of Marines.

On the opposite side of the ship Conex containers packed full of materiel (the military term for equipment and material) belonging to the several companies of Marines were being offloaded. Suspended by taut cables, stretching from the boom of the crane, the room sized steel containers were lifted from the cargo hold to the waiting Mike boats.

Eventually losing interest in watching the seemingly endless parade of Marines exiting the ship, we turned our attention to the offloading of equipment on the other side. On the front of each olive drab container the unit name and platoon number was prominently stenciled in large white letters and numbers.

As our First Sergeant had already confirmed that we were not getting off at Cam Rahn, we were surprised to see the container marked 28TH FINANCE DETACHMENT being offloaded with those belonging to the Marines. As the container swung over the water between the ship and transport vessel, the crane operator saw the stenciling and instantly braked, reversing the direction of the boom. An overstressed cable snapped sending the container with all of our equipment, supplies and thirteen M-14 rifles to the bottom of Cam Rahn Bay.

How could we go on without our equipment and weapons? Was this a game changer? We turned with expectant smiles to our First Sergeant who was standing behind us.

Reflecting our smiles in a moment of uncharacteristic humor he said, "Don't even think that this little SNAFU is y'all's ticket back to the states. Our shit will be replaced by the time y'all crawl off this tub!" Not unlike my grade school teachers, the man could read minds.

The ship was scheduled to leave Cam Rahn Bay that same night, but as the sun set, those of us remaining on deck noticed two rickety motorboats, bearing two occupants each, come alongside, slow nearly to a stop and actually bump gently into the ship. They both sat still in the water for a moment then sped off toward shore.

A sharp eyed member of the ship's security team had been watching the activity, and acted in accordance with protocol by reporting the incident to his commander. Concerned with the unlikely possibility that explosives could have been placed on the side of the ship, the Captain, erring on the side of caution, called for assistance.

Within an hour a team of Navy divers arrived. Visibility was limited as night had fallen, but the lights on the Navy watercraft allowed us to watch as the divers jumped or rolled into the water on either side of the ship.

In the wee hours of the morning the Commander of the diving team announced the all-clear to the ship's Captain. We were not informed as to whether or not explosives were found. Once again we had to assume that we really didn't "need-to-know." Remaining dry and above the water's surface was all that was really important to us even if we were not entrusted with the details of the search. The sun was coming up as the ship began steaming south to our next destination on Vietnam's coast.

****

As my body and mind were becoming more accustomed to the seafaring life, I relaxed on deck and gazed reflectively east at the rippled surface of the South China Sea. My thoughts turned to the events of the previous night and the selfless action of the Navy divers who had come to our aid at the risk of their own safety. I was strangely warmed by what I can best describe as a feeling of patriotic pride and camaraderie at being a small part of a combined military force comprised of individuals willing to endure personal risks to protect their own.

Forty-eight hours later, as the ship entered Vung Tau Bay, the ambient temperature was hot and the humidity sticky. However, concern with atmospheric discomfort faded as our First Sergeant appeared before us wearing a .45 pistol on his hip and announcing that we were finally "home."

Unaware of the logistical magic performed by the armorer at Vung Tau prior to our arrival, we were surprised to be issued new M-14 rifles; replacements for the originals now resting at the bottom of Cam Rahn Bay. It also confirmed our faith in the extrasensory abilities of our First Sergeant.

As I looked over my well-oiled weapon I couldn't help but think, "This can't be a good sign! Are we going to shoot our way ashore?"

Moments later, I asked when we would be issued ammunition, and was told we wouldn't need it anytime soon. That seemed like a good sign – at the time.

Without further delay we grabbed our duffle bags and weapons and began descending the narrow staircase into the waiting "Mike" boats. Fifteen minutes later we climbed awkwardly from the rim of the boat onto a newly built dock that bore evidence of a job completed by the Navy Seabees about an hour before our arrival – with the final nails being hammered in and paint still wet!

Like it or not, we were now "in country."

CHAPTER TWENTY-FIVE

Construction was underway as we arrived at our permanent station. It was like watching a small town grow around us on a mixed base of sandy soil, scrubby bushes, tropical plants and the occasional palm tree. A small, but serviceable air field had been completed to accommodate a growing number of propeller driven airplanes and helicopters. The edge of the tarmac was lined with orange and white striped barrels containing a chemical defoliant known as Agent Orange.

Our first living quarters were comprised of several medium sized tents which were uncomfortably warm during the night and uninhabitable during daylight. Mercifully, construction of our permanent accommodations had begun prior to our arrival and was completed by our twelfth day in country.

Known as a "hootch", the design of the structure was loosely based on that of the thatch roof huts used by the rural Vietnamese. The design differed somewhat from one camp to another, as they were constructed from whatever materials were available to the Engineer Company assigned to each area. Ours was a state-of-the-art construction on a 15'x40' concrete pad. It sported metal screen attached to vertical studs and a large over-hanging roof.

The structure was adequate for keeping the rain off our heads and mosquitos and roaches, for the most part, on the outside. It also kept the rats out…at first. The screened walls allowed the rare enjoyment of an occasional breeze. Access was gained by a latchless screen door on either end of the hootch.

****

I was assigned to the Cash Control area of our Finance unit, and was able to go to work immediately as I did not require the equipment that was necessary for the other sections to operate. The Military Pay section required adding machines and mechanical calculators that had yet to be replaced.

I, along with a Sergeant and one Officer, ran a small disbursing operation in the tiny lobby of a hotel in downtown Vung Tau for the first week while construction of a permanent office building was being completed. The concrete floored, steel building was under roof the following week, just in time for delivery of our new office furniture and equipment. Lacking amenities, including windows, doors, electricity and phones, the structure became a temporary storage shed for the new materiel; raising the next question of how best to secure that equipment?

Me outside the Finance hooch

CHAPTER TWENTY-SIX

As our base was located in a fairly secure area in the coastal region of South Vietnam, the usual military formalities associated with guard duty were unofficially as well as unadvisedly waived. Except for the airfield, security measures were limited to several coils of concertina wire strung loosely around the perimeter of camp. Because our unfinished office was now filled with new furnishings and equipment, the need for a guard was apparent. One of our members, Rico, drew the short straw that first night. His only instructions were to, "Remain inside the building and keep an eye on things."

Rico grew up in a 'burb of New York City, the oldest son of a Puerto Rican family who came there at the close of World War II. Being part of a loving, hard-working family, he acquired his people skills and work ethic first hand. His survival skills were learned on the raw streets of his hometown.

Exuding a quiet confidence, probably the result of having to prove himself in occasional run-ins with young toughs on those streets, he seemed better suited to handle extreme situations than the rest of our unit who had experienced only simulated adversaries during basic training. Maybe that's why he was chosen.

As darkness began to overtake the interior of the building, Rico sought to make his surroundings as comfortable as possible for the duration of, what was expected to be, a long quiet night. Slicing long strips of cardboard from empty shipping cartons, he stacked them on top of a large desk, creating a comparatively soft surface for reclining.

With the only alternative being to stay on his feet and stare into the darkness for the next eight hours, he opted to stretch out on his, less than comfortable, creation. As he laid back he placed his M-14 rifle diagonally across his torso. He intended to stay awake, but sleep soon overtook his tired body.

The first indication that he was not alone in the dark came a few minutes after 2am. One of two intruders bumped against his desk in the pitch blackness and began chattering in Vietnamese to his cohort, completely unaware that Rico was within touching distance.

Remaining quiet and still may have been the best option, but shock and adrenaline took over as Rico bolted straight up, his index finger wrapped tightly around the trigger of his weapon while chambering a round with his free hand. The chambered round exploded with a deafening roar, enhanced by the steel walls of the building, sending the bullet through the roof of the unfinished office.

The intruders ran stumbling through the darkness to the same open window they had used to gain entry. Rico pointed his rifle toward the sounds of their noisy retreat and squeezed the trigger repeatedly – nineteen times in all – until the magazine was spent. He continued squeezing the trigger with no further result.

Rico sat in silence, a death grip on his weapon, trying to sort reality from nightmare until the sirens of Military Police vehicles pierced his trauma impaired hearing. Light flooded the entire area as a squad of Military Police arrived on the scene.

Outside, on the sandy soil beneath the open window, were two dead bodies.

****

If the reason for the intrusion was ever determined, we were never informed. Assumptions ran the gamut from opportunist burglars to mischievous teenaged kids to Viet Cong operatives.

It was determined that Rico had reacted properly in defense of himself and the government property in his charge.

He had no alternative course of action as he was alone, with no communication device, no light and no plan or instruction from his superiors.

As the war intensified throughout Vietnam, this lack of leadership became more evident not only in the support areas, but more specifically, in areas of direct and frequent combat. Inexperience and indecision on the part of ill-prepared and poorly trained officers resulted in the unnecessary deaths of young soldiers under their command. In areas of more intense combat this epidemic of incompetence led to incidents of vigilante retribution known as "fragging."

CHAPTER TWENTY-SEVEN

The entire incident involving Rico provided a lesson rich experience for the officers and men of our small unit. The oft quoted axiom, "We learn from our mistakes," was certainly applicable. In some ways we did.

Security lighting became a priority, guard duty was expanded to a two man operation, and the creation of a local protocol for handling exceptional situations was ordered. A phone system was on order, but we were standing in line for that popular service.

With the break-in still foremost on the minds and agenda of our inexperienced officer staff, we were cautioned in an ambiguous manner, "Avoid the use of lethal force and analyze each special situation to determine with whom we were dealing."

The well worded directive was no doubt intended to prevent any further deaths of innocent locals who might wonder into our office in the wee hours of the morning, but unfortunately lacked any details regarding implementation.

****

Three days later, but prior to the completion of the new protocol, I was assigned nighttime guard duty at the office. I reasoned that, even if completed, the new procedures would have been written in the usual unintelligible military jargon, rendering them nearly useless anyway.

Construction of our new office had reached completion with the installation of the windows and doors. Electric service had been extended from the base power plant. Security lighting – so called due to its intended purpose rather than actual function – was hung from the four outside corners of the building. Inadequate wattage and shadowy voids completed the well intentioned, though deficient, attempt at illuminating the perimeter of the building. Telephone service remained on the wish list.

Newly established Standard Operating Procedure for the night watch at the office, as explained by the First Sergeant, would be to keep the interior of the building completely dark to minimize the possibility of being shot at through the windows. This seemed like a sensible strategy to me as I recalled the ease with which I used to shoot the little metal ducks in the brightly lit shooting gallery at the annual Tuscarawas County Fair. (Growing older and wiser, I eventually realized that I was purchasing the stuffed bear prize and getting to shoot for free).

Now it was my turn to spend a sleepless night guarding the government property that had been strategically arranged in a standardized military format for office furniture. Darkness overtook the camp as I went about the task of assuring myself that I could see out and no one could see in.

Satisfied, I settled into a squeaky office chair behind a dull gray desk with my back to the steel wall of the building. Recalling the plight of one of my childhood heroes, Wild Bill Hickok, who had been shot in the back in a Deadwood, South Dakota saloon for failing to do that very thing, I felt somewhat safer taking the extra precaution.

Flicking on a cumbersome Army issue D cell flashlight and adjusting the diffuser lens to allow just enough light to illuminate a small area of desktop, I began to write the first of several letters home.

****

Except for dire emergencies, letters were the only available means of communication with loved ones back home, but using the Army Post Office was a slow process. Had the term "snail mail" existed at the time, it would have taken on a more profound meaning in 1966 Vietnam.

Fourteen days elapsed between a question asked and an answer received or between receiving news of a death in the family and sending a sincere, "I'm so sorry to hear that," or between sending a heartfelt, " I love you" and receiving a heartfelt, "I love you" in response – fourteen frustrating days.

****

It was just after 1:00am when I sensed movement outside the far end of the building. I looked up to see six small figures with weapons strapped to their backs, their single file progress dimly silhouetted against a distant security light. Seconds later the door rattled as the first man, obviously the leader, tried to turn the locked door knob. A few words of mumbled Vietnamese preceded a dull thud as a pry bar was forced into the door jamb followed by the retching sound of metal being mangled. The door popped open!

As my heart thudded, I flicked off the dim flashlight and quietly lifted the .45 caliber pistol from the holster resting against my right leg. Holding the weapon in my lap I sat perfectly still…except for some mild involuntary shaking.

The Captain's words echoed in my stress induced thoughts, "analyze situation – no lethal force – who are you dealing with?"

Having no heroic leanings at the moment and lacking the inclination to protect government property at the cost of human life, especially mine, I was hoping to sit this one out. It was soon apparent that hope was not an applicable strategy in this situation.

The would-be raiding party must have been confident of finding the darkened building vacant, as they entered with weapons still slung over their shoulders. The leader flicked a cigarette lighter and held it over his head, providing a surprising amount of illumination to the darkened interior of the office. The light reflected off the faces of the motley band huddled around him. Dressed in soiled street clothes they appeared to be in their mid-teens. The leader was probably thirty.

What to do? One possible course of action after another was rejected as soon as it came to mind. Thoughts came in rapid succession: Are these guys Viet Cong, or just locals looking to make a score? They have guns! They broke in! They don't have uniforms! Then in that dreaded, "Why me" moment …"Oh shit, they see me!"

In one of those unexplainable actions that you know you're going to regret as soon as you hear yourself say the words, I reverted to my previous customer service training in banking and asked, "May I help you?"

As the question echoed in my head and I questioned my sanity, the leader responded in broken English, "Oh, GI, we want ceegaretts."

Dialogue, even with conspicuously armed burglars, is always an ice breaker and seemed to ease the tension of the moment. I said, in a slightly relaxed tone, "Sorry, I don't have cigarettes."

The group followed his lead as he drifted slowly toward me and repeated his request for cigarettes. Stopping about four feet in front of my desk he sneered with a condescending smile and nodded to his gang members standing on either side. They responded with their own nod, returned the leader's grin and began moving toward me while reaching for the sling of their weapons.

In the next adrenaline infused moment I realized that this rag-tag street gang was about to stand in the way of me ever leaving this God forsaken battle zone, and returning to my girl, my family and my future. I had to act!!

Refusing to be a part of their agenda I squeezed my weapon in a death grip, bolted from the chair and cocked the hammer as I shoved it point blank in the leader's face. From my very limited Vietnamese vocabulary I shouted," Dung lai!"

Still holding the burning Zippo lighter, the leader raised both hands in a mock sign of surrender and crooned, in a syrupy tone, "Whoa, be nice GI. We just want ceegarettes."

A split second later the familiar clack of a round being chambered in an M-14 rifle echoed off the steel walls of the building accompanied by a booming command, "EVERYBODY, STAND THE F- - - STILL!" The volume and inflection was more than enough to transcend any language barrier. I couldn't have been happier if the U.S. Army Band had marched through that broken door playing THE STARS AND STRIPES FOREVER!

In all the excitement I had forgotten that I wasn't alone. My foul-mouthed fellow guard had been asleep in the vault room and was now standing in the doorway behind the intruders with his rifle leveled at their backs. The instant warmth of relief radiating through my body was interrupted, as I flicked on my dim flashlight, revealing that I was, along with our uninvited guests, at the muzzle end of my partner's rifle. I stepped gingerly to the right while keeping the pistol pointed at the leader's head.

My fellow guard and I had a hushed discussion regarding what to do with our prisoners who were, by then, sitting on the floor with hands behind their heads. In light of the ambiguous unwritten directive, not to mention our inability to contact the Military Police on the opposite side of the base, we decided to let them go!

During a brief exchange of words, which I could only assume contained some heartfelt Vietnamese profanity my partner issued his own expletive rich instructions to our prisoners regarding their evacuation of the building.

We escorted them out of the building and watched as they climbed single file along a large wooden plank they had used to smash down the concertina wire (our security fence) to gain entrance to the camp.

Assured that our visitors were outside the compound, we secured the broken door by jamming a desk against it then proceeded to clear our weapons to avoid the possibility of accidental discharge. My partner removed the magazine from his rifle and ejected the unfired round.

Following suit I removed the magazine from my pistol and retracted the slide to eject the unfired round…nothing came out! The chamber was empty! I had survived my first potentially lethal encounter with armed adversaries with no cartridge in the chamber of my weapon!

A short mental parade of "What if" scenarios followed. What if I had been forced to squeeze the trigger? The feeble click of the hammer dropping behind an empty chamber could have earned my partner and me Purple Hearts and/or body bags! What if my partner wouldn't have been roused from his sleep? Same result.

As it sometimes does, my mind involuntarily flashed back to thoughts of a particular Sunday school lesson when, as an eight-year-old, I learned of David the shepherd boy's fight with Goliath. I was appalled that David had come to the most important confrontation of his life without stones for his sling, and had to search the ground around him for ammo.

That particular flashback only served to make me feel worse about my own lack of preparation. At least David had a stone in the pouch of his sling, and he was a better shot with his homemade sling than I was with my state-of-the-art weapon.

Rationalization was the next float in the parade, providing ample excuses for my oversight. First, I blamed the Army for insufficient training with my weapon. Continued weapons training for members of the Finance Corps was woefully inadequate.

My blame shifting continued, as I recalled that the one and only time I had fired a .45 pistol was during the initial familiarization exercise at Camp des Loges the previous year...

****

I was standing in a single file line immediately behind the unit commander at the pistol range. The Colonel, who was nearing his date of retirement, was the first to shoot at the one square foot target that was affixed to a back stop fifteen yards in front of the firing line. When he had completed his required twenty-one shots (three magazines) he turned to me and said, "Well son, you might as well use my target 'cause I sure as hell didn't do it any damage."

I don't remember how well I did, but the target looked fairly intact when I had completed firing the mandatory three magazines.

****

I assumed that the scant training provided was due to a presumed low probability of Finance Corps personnel ever being in an armed confrontation. It was an assumption that I subconsciously carried with me to Vietnam.

My parade of excuses ended with a self-imposed slap in the face, and unconditional acceptance of personal responsibility for what could have happened. I resolved to change my attitude and level of preparedness.

Surviving the events of that night was either dumb luck or providence. On the off chance that it was the latter I silently thanked God for the intervention.

The following morning we were lectured by our Captain who reviewed for us our mistakes and really bad choices of the previous evening. To our welcome surprise, the mild upbraiding was moderated even further by his acceptance of the ultimate responsibility for our lack of instruction and inability to contact the MPs. (Through some military hocus-pocus, telephones were installed the next day).

I didn't relate to him the details regarding my weapon nor did we share with the rest of our unit the context of our conversation with the Captain.

The remainder of that day was business as usual at the office, but I faced the day with a new imperative – personal responsibility required an action plan…

CHAPTER TWENTY-EIGHT

The events of those first few weeks in our new office caused me to question the effectiveness of our security measures, not only at our work place, but our living quarters as well. The openness of our tropical styled structure made it accessible to anyone, friend or foe, twenty-four hours a day- eight of which our eyes were closed!

Further aggravating my new obsession with security, I held the dubious honor of being in charge of our open air barracks; a responsibility that required me to occupy an enclosed cubicle, located immediately inside the screen door that faced our "security fence."

My concern for our security wasn't shared by most of the unit. I could understand their indifference as they had been "in country" for several weeks without being shot at and much of their initial apprehension had faded. The general assumption was that someone else on the perimeter of the camp was watching out for them. That assumption hadn't worked well for Rico or me.

Even in a designated combat area there is a tendency for troops in support positions – that is, not directly involved in combat operations, to take their personal security for granted. Besides, with thirteen comrades in the same big room with an ample supply of beer, what was there to worry about?

Adding to this complacent attitude was the near presence of a contingent of the Korean Tiger Division. Reputed to be fierce fighters and willingly ruthless in the execution of their duty, they were feared and respected by the Viet Cong who opted for avoidance rather than confrontation if the option existed.

An example of that ruthlessness was graphically displayed

near the gate of the Korean Camp. Four of us were en route to exchange currency for an incoming troop ship. As we neared the Tiger compound we saw what looked like a gutted deer hanging upside down in a tree. As our jeep neared the grizzly sight we saw that it was not a deer, but a mutilated human body. Maybe he was a captured Viet Cong or maybe a local thief, but certainly a terrible but effective example of why they were feared.

In addition to being welcomed with open arms by the governments of South Vietnam as well as America, Korean soldiers received special benefits from the South Korean government for volunteering for duty in Vietnam. They enjoyed unlimited access to, and use of, our base and facilities without the limitations we were required to observe. This led to Korean soldiers making excessive purchases at our Post Exchange of electronics, alcohol, clothing and food items which were then sold on the burgeoning black market for substantial profit.

****

With our immediate security at the hootch still dependent on a roll of unattended concertina wire and no apparent remedy in sight, I formed my own plan for nighttime security.

Being the head cashier, I was armed each work day with a .45 caliber pistol. At the end of each day I placed it under a shelf in the barred enclosure that served as my work station. Securing my weapon in this manner was part of my daily routine, but I had no specific instructions to do so. It simply seemed the proper thing to do rather than to leave it lie exposed on the counter of my work space. Early on, the day to day operation of our newly formed finance unit was a work-in-progress. Guidelines existed, but trial, error and innovation were the general business model.

Being armed during the work day, for the purpose of protecting government currency seemed far less important to me than being armed during the dark of night to prevent throat slitting by an enemy who, by recent example, seemed to have random access to our camp.

I considered running my idea past our irresolute officer staff, but drawing on previous experience with complacent officers who were comfortable with the status quo, I rejected the notion. Any innovation or procedural change in the Vietnam era military environment invariably came from the top down. I had to assume that an idea to improve security coming from an E-5 pay grade enlisted man would have less than a snowball's chance of being approved. Had I requested permission to implement my plan, been refused and acted anyway, I would have most likely received a reprimand or wound up in jail.

In the final analysis, I knew it was just too important to leave my personal safety and that of my hootch-mates to the preoccupied attention of our immediate superiors who, like many other officers, lived off-post in a tightly guarded facility. My concern was genuine and the need, as I saw it, was immediate.

At the close of business the following day, instead of securing my weapon as usual, I tucked it into my waistband beneath the shirt of my fatigue uniform. The proverbial rubber had met the road and it was sobering. I had never violated an established procedure or order, but there was no written directive specifically limiting possession of my assigned weapon after work hours.

Rationalization of my decision was supported by the limited legal knowledge I had gained in a commercial law class the previous year, part of which, reviewed the limitations of "implied contracts." In my very shaky legal opinion, implied policies, or the absence thereof, shouldn't prevent my action, and were trumped by common sense and the innate right of survival. That, and that alone, would be my anemic defense should my action be discovered. Right or wrong, I was taking my former Finance Officer's advice by using what education I had received and not wasting it.

Completing my mental list of justifications, I knew that my cause was righteous and necessary, and I would see it through because no one, including myself, was going to die needlessly on my unsanctioned watch. With that mental wrestling match won, I left the office and walked to the hootch with the warm assurance that I was doing the right thing.

In the hootch, my cubicle offered enough privacy for me to move my weapon from concealment in my waistband to the footlocker adjacent to my cot and ultimately to its nighttime location under my pillow. Through practice I became proficient at field stripping, reassembling and dry firing my weapon to the point of performing those functions in pitch blackness. Of course, all practice was done with my weapon unloaded. Dry firing wasn't a common practice in 1966, but became the go to, affordable familiarization exercise decades later when the concealed carry culture emerged.

Within six weeks, after several more breaching incidents, Military Police presence was increased and overall security beefed-up making my precautions less critical. None of those incidents had occurred in the near area of our hootch during the course of my volunteer security initiative, but I felt justified in having been prepared should the worst have happened. I was not concerned, and indeed thankful, that my unauthorized, unappreciated, and of utmost importance, undiscovered plan was not needed.

I could now relax and let the MPs do their job. My watch had ended, but in that short time I had grown accustomed to having my weapon constantly within reach, and found it impossible to go to sleep without it. Thus, my assigned weapon, a World War II era Remington Rand .45 caliber pistol, remained in a holster on my right hip or inside my fatigue shirt or under my pillow until the morning I boarded a Caribou bound for Ton Son Nhut airbase and home.

CHAPTER TWENTY-NINE

My obsession with personal security, and the security of my hootch-mates, had been somewhat placated the previous month by the increased presence of Military Police. Prior to that increase, the number of breaching incidents was on the rise.

As the Military Police finally had a handle on camp security, I felt deserving of the brief respite from my self-imposed shepherding duties. Approaching the end of my short military career, and having experienced the uncertainty that accompanies military life, I should have known better than to expect this positive turn of events to last.

No sooner had I put to rest the very possible concern of having our throats slit during the night by a bona fide enemy, than a more sinister threat from our own ranks loomed. The only difference this time was that my hootch-mates were in no danger – the problem was mine alone.

As head cashier I processed most ordinary cash transactions and all exceptional cash transfers, disbursements and deposits through my work station. Cash disbursements made up ninety-nine percent of daily transactions. Deposits were rare; that is, until a new officer transferred into our unit.

A young officer, who had recently graduated from a college ROTC program, came to us with his shiny new insignia of rank on a starched collar, an arrogant attitude and a dysfunctional moral compass; not a good combination in a war zone rife with black market activity, drug trafficking and a tempting array of nefarious money making opportunities.

Our Captain and Executive Officer were scheduled for a thirty day temporary duty assignment in Saigon, and the new officer was to handle official duties during their absence. It was a day or so after their departure that I was presented with the first of several deposits in unusually large amounts by one of two Captains who claimed to be stationed at units located quite a distance from our area.

I tried to explain to the first of the pair that deposits made to the type of investment account he was requesting had to be funded with income earned while in a combat zone. Given the large amount, he would have had to be "in country" since childhood! Aside from the amount, the transaction bore the earmarks of an attempt to launder proceeds from drug or black market sales. I reported the activity to our new officer who told me not to concern myself with it and that he would handle it.

A similar transaction the next day by the other officer required a validating signature so I referred it to the new officer who told me to sign it myself. I told him that I wasn't comfortable signing it as I could not determine the origin of the funds.

Becoming agitated with the delay, the Captain stormed into the office behind me. The new officer glanced up at him, leaned half-way across his desk and in a hushed, snarling tone said, "I don't care about your damned comfort level, sign the form! That's a direct order, Specialist!"

I turned to see the victorious sneer on the Captain's face and said, "Sorry for the delay, Sir," and signed the authorization.

Their glances at each other confirmed what I had feared – they were not strangers.

Similar transactions occurred over the next three weeks and I processed and signed all of them without further questions. It grated on me to do so, but I was following orders, albeit reluctantly. I had no one to turn to at the moment, and felt that the best course of action was to do as told until the Company Commander returned.

But things were about to take a bizarre turn.

The new officer lived off-post in the same guarded facility as the other officers, so it was totally unexpected when he burst into the office in mid-afternoon looking like he had seen a ghost, and ordered several of us to start building a bunker in the company commander's office.

Thinking it was a joke, a couple of the guys started laughing until he flew into them in a rage. The only plausible explanation was that he had crossed the wrong people downtown – maybe an unpaid gambling debt, a drug deal gone bad or any number of other corrupt scenarios.

Next, he instructed two of us to draw our weapons from the rack, load them and be prepared to stand guard over him as he slept. He was either totally clueless or so deeply embedded in his own arrogance that he couldn't see that he was pissing-off the very people he was counting on to protect him!

As strange as it seemed to us, we did as ordered and began building a bunker large enough to accommodate a cot. Sandbags were plentiful and within easy reach as a small crew of locals had been at work for several days sandbagging the exterior of our office building.

As we worked, the men were speculating as to the cause of the new officer's erratic behavior and openly complaining

Sandbags were plentiful

about pulling extra duty for his benefit. Doing more listening than contributing to the rantings of my coworkers, I began to get the uneasy feeling that I knew, better than they, the answer.

His personal problem didn't concern me at first. Actually, it was somewhat gratifying to witness his arrogant demeanor shrivel to cold-sweat cowardice; gratifying, that is, until I began to isolate the most likely reason for his concern.

****

Filling sandbags was mindless work and allowed ample time to mentally entertain a chain of "What if" scenarios, each more disturbing than the preceding:

What if it wasn't a threat from a disgruntled gambler, drug dealer or black-market operator that was scaring him?

What if it were one or more of his back-slapping buddies who had been frequenting the office with money from who knows where?

What if our new officer had gotten cold feet and wanted out or, more in keeping with his unbounded arrogance, demanded a larger cut of the take?

Then it hit me like the proverbial ton of bricks. They knew that it was I who had recognized and attempted to interfere with their enterprise. At this point I didn't know who was included in "they." I had not mentioned a word to anyone other than the new officer and that was causing me enough grief.

The "What if" scenarios continued:

What if their illegal activities were discovered by someone else? Would an investigation implicate me?

How would I explain my signature on the only documents related to their scam?

"I was just following orders," might seem a weak defense at a Court Martial.

Am I bound to follow an order that I feel may be illegal or immoral?

I had gone everywhere the Army sent me, and I would go anywhere I was told, but the Federal Prison at Fort Leavenworth was not on my preferred assignment list!

It got worse…

My emotional state vacillated between denial that anything actually illegal was happening, and a chilling, lonely anxiety because I knew it was. Unshakable concern morphed into paranoia as I began to wonder if I had seen enough to be considered a risk, and maybe even expendable by the involved parties? Any doubts I had that I was in the middle of something bad were dispelled by the new officer's erratic behavior.

Being thousands of miles from home in the most hostile environment of my life, and alone in the knowledge of illegitimate activity I wasn't sure whom to trust or where to turn. I just wanted the Commander to get back so I could unload this on him…but what if he were one of them?

****

A few days later the Commander and Executive Officer returned from Saigon. Upon entering his office, the Commander demanded to know the reason for the bunker. Shortly we were dismantling the ill-conceived structure while eavesdropping to hear our officer being instructed as to the Commander's expectations regarding his future.

Even with things returning to a reasonable semblance of normal, I was still hesitant to speak with the Commander about the happenings of the past thirty days. I still simply didn't know whom to trust.

Although the suspicious transactions stopped abruptly with the return of the regular officer staff, I still felt uneasy about doing my job every day. With only a few months remaining till my tour of duty was complete I felt it best to distance myself from the possibility of any questionable activity, should it resume. To that end, I requested a transfer from the Cash Control section to the Military Pay section. My request was denied.

****

I don't know what happened to the new officer. I never saw him again and that was fine with me.

But now I was at a moral juncture. What to do? Should I tell what I knew or keep my mouth shut? Prior to this point in my life, decisions weren't hard to make:

If I couldn't afford it, I didn't buy it. If I found it and it wasn't mine, I tried to find the rightful owner. If I didn't see a cop, I ignored the posted speed limit. If I loved the girl and couldn't live without her, I asked her to marry me.

It used to be easy. But after these events, black and white had become diluted.

I knew the proper course of action would be to follow the chain-of-command and report the wrong doing, but if I told the wrong people, I might go home in a body bag; ostensibly a hero, but actually just a quixotic, do-good fool.

And then, why should I even care about the government's money? God knows that government waste of taxpayer money, valuable resources and precious lives was rampant. In comparison, my discovery was peanuts. What would be gained by reporting black market activity that has survived every war known to mankind, or drug trafficking which was fast becoming an epidemic? What about the lives of innocent Asian girls sold or cajoled into prostitution, a profitable industry that my own fellow soldiers were helping to perpetuate? What could I do about any of it anyway?

My thoughts were jumbled and chaining too fast. I had to put this whole sordid mess into a proper perspective. My only priority was to survive the next few months and go home. Exposing corrupt behavior wasn't going to gain me anything but grief. This wasn't one of those war-time scenes where I heroically save a buddy by falling on a grenade! I would be saving nothing by reporting what I knew.

I was so tired of thinking, so tired of worrying, that my constant apprehension turned to a teeth gritting, pissed off determination to survive. At the end of the work day, I jammed my .45 into my waistband with more purpose than usual and walked back to the hootch with a new outlook, and no intention of dying in this tropical hell. Screw the new officer, screw his crooked associates, and screw trying to save the government's money!

It didn't matter to me anymore if they thought I knew too much. I was not going to be a part of their agenda! If worse came to worst I would defend myself however necessary. I would rather explain my actions at a Court Martial than burden a fellow soldier assigned to Graves Registration with another lifeless body- least of all mine.

CHAPTER THIRTY

I attempted to put my constant state of alertness on a mental back burner, but the urge to look over my shoulder and sleep with one eye open remained a day and night ritual. The possibility of my nemesis returning to tie up any lose ends may not have been probable, but it occupied that back burner and was never completely out of my thoughts.

Being assigned to a support group carried less risk than being in the field with a high probability of direct contact with the enemy. However, references such as, "On the front line" or "Away from the front line", belonged to another war, and lost meaning in Vietnam, as there were usually no defined "lines". There never has been, or ever will be, a lack of potential hazards in a war zone.

Bullets, rockets, and other assorted flying metals weren't the only dangers to be avoided in Vietnam. Punji sticks and various home-spun weapons were a part of the enemy's arsenal. Even human and animal waste became an occasional go to weapon of the resourceful Viet Cong who used them to inflict infection or illness on their enemies.

A more insidious danger was the intentional, as well as, accidental contact with a tactical weapon used by our own troops against the Viet Cong. Inflicting immediate damage to the enemy's operational ability, it also caused the eventual illness, and often death of those who handled or were unknowingly exposed to the chemical known as Agent Orange.

Agent Orange is defined as an herbicide and defoliant for tactical use. It was sprayed from specially equipped airplanes and helicopters, in heavy concentrations, to eliminate trees and underbrush being used by the Viet Cong for cover.

Perhaps the most bizarre method of accidental contact with

the toxic defoliant was while using the latrine…the head…the outhouse!

On our base, the most commonly found facility was a four seat outhouse. The "seats" were actually just four dinner plate sized holes cut into a well-sanded board, and referred to as seats because they were sat upon. The wooden outhouses were, most often, centrally located in the midst of the conglomeration of hootches.

They lacked amenities – after the first use one remembered one's toilet paper – as well as privacy. Personally, I sought the moments of lowest usage for my daily ritual, but readily overcame my desire for privacy if necessity prevailed.

In addition to the four holes of obvious function, there was a four foot long tube, eight inches in diameter, protruding from the sandy soil to a height of twenty-four inches, with the remaining twenty-four inches below ground level. Referred to as a "relief tube" its function was also obvious.

The number of troops availing themselves of the facilities on a daily basis necessitated an efficient method of disposal – enter the "Shit Barrels." These were repurposed fifty-five gallon containers that had been cut in half, providing two receptacles for…well…uh, use in the outhouse. Handles were welded on either side to facilitate insertion under the aforementioned holes. Extraction of the barrels was performed each evening when, with the addition of diesel fuel and a tiny quantity of gasoline, they were ignited, their contents burning into the nighttime sky. When cooled they were reinserted for use the next day. Those barrels originally contained Agent Orange as testified to by the circumferential orange and white stripes painted on them.

****

On one memorable evening, a new member of our unit was assigned to over-night guard duty at the office. This being his first time, he nervously reviewed the check list of chores with his fellow guard to be sure all procedures would be completed as required.

As the new guy, he was given the less desirable jobs on the list, the first of which was to burn the poop barrels. At the proper hour he gathered all the necessary elements to complete the task and proceeded dutifully toward the outhouse located about thirty yards from the office.

Gingerly pulling the barrels from beneath the two-hole outhouse, he dragged them the prescribed twenty feet away from the facility, and began emptying a five gallon can of gasoline, in equal amounts, into each barrel. He topped off the mixture with a splash of kerosene - the exact opposite of the required amount of each fuel!

Providence or dumb luck caused him to return to the outhouse where he lit a tightly rolled copy of The Army Times newspaper and tossed it, bean bag style, at the nearest barrel. Before the flaming newspaper was half way to the target, the vapors ignited sending the contents of the barrels skyward!

Fortunately, he was far enough away to only singe eyebrows and arm hair. Unfortunately, the stuff came back down in a wide random pattern!

****

I'm unsure as to whether the toxic residue in the empty barrels was mitigated in the burning process, or widely distributed into the air, but every night as the smoke billowed from the barrels, it loomed in a dull yellow-gray haze in the near atmosphere above the camp.

Our prescribed method of waste disposal was probably the most expedient at the time and no one came forward to suggest a better option.

I've often wondered if the subsequent rash of physical maladies blamed on exposure to Agent Orange was based on actual contact with the liquid form, or from inhaling the vaporized mist sprayed from planes, or from breathing, during the night, the smoky product of the burning barrels.

****

As we would soon discover, contact with Agent Orange was only one of the imperceptible dangers posed to everyone with boots on the ground in Vietnam…

Agent Orange Barrels

CHAPTER THIRTY-ONE

The last traces of smoke from Saturday night's smoldering barrels had dissipated in a rare offshore breeze, and Sunday morning dawned with an uncommon pleasantness; warm rather than hot, with humidity at an acceptable level. As on every previous Sunday, the office was closed except for the Cash Control section. My assistant cashier and I worked alternate Sundays with another team, and on this beautiful day it was our turn.

Vung Tau beach was calling, and most of the office staff answered the call by donning swim trunks and jumping on the first available deuce-and-a-half truck bound for the bay area. They happily shared the burden of carrying several coolers filled with beer and sodas, as well as a variety of picnic edibles purloined from the mess hall, with the help of a sympathetic member of the mess hall staff.

Late that afternoon the sunburned horde returned to camp. Working in an office six days a week hadn't prepared them for a full day in the sun, and sunscreen was an unknown commodity. A couple thoughtful members brought left-over food and drink to the office for our enjoyment. I was appreciative of their kindness, and proceeded to munch on the hot dogs that had cooled, the potato salad that had warmed, some potato chip crumbs and a can of warm soda. All of the beer had been consumed by the party-goers while it was still cold. My fellow cashier declined their kindness as he had just eaten at the mess hall…all the better for him.

****

In the early morning darkness we were jarred awake by

the sounds of retching, and slamming screen doors as one after the other of my hootch-mates ran, crawled and lunged through both exits clambering to the nearest outhouse!

Except for the rude awakening, I felt perfectly fine and wondered what communicable malady had hit them so quickly. Had they been gassed and if so, how was I missed?

They were all taken to the base hospital for testing and observation. Four of us were unaffected, and it didn't take long to determine that our avoidance of the sickness may have been due to our avoidance of the beach party.

About five hours later, bent over with unprecedented pain, I joined my brethren at the base hospital with the same symptoms. The early diagnosis was food poisoning – probably the potato salad. However, cultures sent to Saigon for analysis told a different story with a war zone twist.

The test results identified the parasitic culprit as Giardia – an infection that is most frequently acquired through ingestion of food or water that is tainted by the feces of an infected human or animal.

The local faction of the Viet Cong had both the ability and opportunity to contaminate the unattended picnic fare, as my fellow soldiers frolicked at the beach on their day off. The usual application of this homespun biological attack was to smear infected feces on sharpened points of punji sticks, and place them where an enemy might step or fall on them. It didn't take a degree in biological science to prepare and lace an unattended table of food with the stuff. One would think that a foul taste would have been detected, but this as well as most mess hall food, was not "home cooking" and the pervading taste of heavily chlorinated water dulled the palate.

Most of the unit recovered in five days and returned to duty. At the same point I had survived the vomiting, diarrhea and dehydration only to begin intestinal bleeding. The medical assumption of the Army doctor was that the pathogen had at least an extra five hours on Sunday to develop before I ingested it. The rest of the unit had picnicked at noon.

The bleeding continued for two more weeks during which

my treatment was limited to a daily visit by my assigned doctor, who stopped at the foot of my cot every day at noon, to ask if I was still bleeding. Each day I answered, "Yes" and he responded," I'll check on you tomorrow," as he headed for a long, laugh punctuated conversation with the very attractive head-nurse.

The base hospital was comprised of a series of eighty-bed Quonset huts. In our hut, there was a screen door on either end. A large fan placed at the west door exhausted the heated air that it drew in through the east door. I was, nevertheless, grateful for the ventilation – even hot air that moves is better than stagnant air that allows one to cook in one's sweat.

Unabated boredom fostered fond thoughts of returning to my cozy work station in the Cash Control section, but my desire to leave the hospital became even more urgent on day fourteen as the patient demographic changed from troops with sundry maladies, to an influx of the victims of a hepatitis outbreak. Within three days the eighty bed building was occupied by seventy-nine hepatitis patients - and me!

The infection apparently having run its course, the bleeding stopped on the twenty-first day and I was dismissed to return to work. Fifteen pounds lighter and somewhat weaker, I walked the quarter mile between the hospital and the office. Entering my barred cashier's cage, I promptly passed-out, only to be abruptly returned to consciousness a minute later as an ammonia capsule was crushed under my nose! The caustic odor caused me to jerk away striking the back of my head against the gate of my steel cage, and bleeding began again, but this time from my head rather than my intestines. A generous dab of antibiotic cream, and several layers of gauze wrapped around my aching head completed my treatment, and I was helped to my feet to continue my first day back to work.

****

In considering my twenty-one days of convalescence at the base hospital, and in complete fairness to my doctor, there was no effective treatment for Giardia available at that time, and I don't blame him at all for spending more time at the nurse's station than with his sweaty patients – she was a knockout with her short blonde hair, blue eyes and tailored fatigues.

CHAPTER THIRTY-TWO

Communication within the military uses several avenues to send and receive information. Some of the most often used forms include an alphabetic code used in semaphore, the phonetic alphabet and the subject of this chapter, the ingenious acronym.

The essence of an acronym is to say a lot by not saying a lot. Some are inappropriate for unrestricted usage, but within the confines of military life, and even some businesses, they are generally accepted. The acronym SNAFU is no exception, and is one of the most commonly used. As nearly as can be determined, it was coined by some creative Marines in World War II to describe the recurring screw-ups that are an inevitable part of military life.

SITUATION NORMAL ALL FOULED UP would be a socially acceptable definition. However, depending on your level of comfort with profanity, you may or may not insert a different "F" word to confront the acronym in its original form.

Characteristically, a SNAFU will occur at the most inconvenient times.

Thus it happened that I was required to fly to Saigon (now Ho Chi Minh City) to obtain the signature of a high ranking official on a time-sensitive document. The missing signature was apparently critical enough to cause my resident officers sufficient vexation to pull me from my usual duty for the task. The part of the scenario that I would prefer to forget is that I, personally, had failed to obtain the signature! In keeping with my policy of fixing my own mistakes, I didn't balk at being sent.

Accordingly, I hopped on a Saigon-bound C-123 – a very large, very loud cargo plane – on a hot, always hot, morning with instructions to get there, get it done and get back.

I took the first seat on a bench affixed to the wall of the plane facing the only other passenger who was sitting on the opposite side of the empty cargo area.

As the bulky aircraft lumbered to the end of the tarmac, I found a length of rope dangling with a carabiner attached to the free end. Pulling it diagonally across me I searched for something to clip it to. My fellow passenger did likewise thereby securing ourselves to our respective benches. It was a mid-1960s military version of a seat-belt.

The plane pivoted abruptly at the end of the runway. There were no windows in the vast cargo area, but I could sense the direction of the plane's movement by being jostled front to back and left to right. After a brief moment of idling, the engines were throttled to a deafening roar and our spacious room rolled forward. We covered our ears attempting to protect our hearing. The vibration of the giant tires rolling on the tarmac soon ceased, confirming that we were airborne. The conversation I intended to initiate with my travel partner was no longer an option. Even as the engines slowed to cruising speed the constant drone made verbal communication impossible.

The sixty air miles to Saigon made for a short flight time. As soon as the aircraft came to a stop at Tan Son Nuht Airbase and the large loading ramp was lowered I exited the rear of the aircraft to begin the search for my prearranged ride.

A Jeep met me at the edge of the runway and I was on my way to the newly completed MACV HQ (Military Assistance Command-Viet Nam Head Quarters) located immediately adjacent to the airbase. The driver said he would wait while I completed my task. I was directed to the office of the official whose signature I needed, only to find that he was called out of the office and wouldn't return until the next morning. SNAFU #1.

I explained my problem to the driver who assured me that there was no problem. He would arrange for me to stay with him at the enlisted men's barracks, which were located within the confines of the airbase. With no better option, I accepted his hospitable offer. We grabbed chow, and I was about to relax and read my way through the afternoon when my overachieving host offered to show me the sights of Saigon. I politely declined, but found that he had already requested special permission from his company commander to show this boy from the boondocks of Vietnam the big city.

As we exited through the main gate of the airbase, my guide motioned to one of many open air taxis, or at least the Vietnamese idea of an open air taxi. The one he chose for us resembled a rickshaw that may have been a motorbike in a former life. The passenger area of this Rube Goldberg designed death trap consisted of a bench type seat attached to the very front, with barely enough room for our two American sized butts. Sitting, or rather perching, on the beltless bench, our knees occupied the space where a front bumper should have been. The only solace I could glean was in finding that the underpowered, two-cycle engine propelling this contraption had a top speed of only seventeen miles per hour.

Traffic was heavy, with small vehicles and large Army trucks passing us from both directions. Even with my precarious bird's eye view, I detected no definable traffic lane. Weaving in and out of the ever changing first come, first served traffic right of way, we were passing bicycles and being passed by anything faster than us, making our exposed position on the front of this wheeled nightmare seem all the more dangerous. Oddly, my guide was fairly calm - no - more distracted than calm. He hadn't said a word since our taxi pulled away from the gate and continued to stare ahead, mindless of our surroundings.

As we arrived at what I assumed was the first stop on our tour, I soon sensed that another eyes open nightmare might be developing. My partner jumped off the bench and started walking away as the driver loudly demanded payment. He turned, and they began dickering about the amount of the fare. Within a few seconds we were surrounded by a host of other drivers who were attracted by the dispute. Finally, my friend crumbled up a 100 piaster note (one fifth of the amount the driver had demanded) and threw it at the driver. Then grabbing my arm, he pulled me toward a nightclub.

I cautioned him about burning bridges that we might need later, but he had already begun to transition from a gracious host to a driven creature –in the "Jeckyll and Hyde" sense. SNAFU #2

We entered the spacious bar where midafternoon clientele were getting an early start on the evening. Uniformed military personnel, as well as many in street clothes, mingled with local civilians. My "guide" instructed me to get a beer and wait for him as he ran up a wide staircase to the second floor to purchase drugs, booze and what turned out to be an hour with a prostitute. It was clear that I had been his ticket to get off base for the night.

The music was loud, the crowd inebriated and the entertainment, two scantily-clad dancers on a raised platform, were exhibiting everything, but talent. An hour had passed and my eyes were fixed on the staircase as I awaited the return of my erstwhile host.

A sleazy looking pair of Asian men in tailored suits, accompanied by several provocatively dressed teenage girls, worked the crowd. If I had any doubt that I was watching pimps at work, it was dispelled when one of them asked me if I would like to spend an hour with one of his, "ree nice girl."

I resisted the urge to crack their tiny heads together, and walked away as he loudly questioned my manhood in severely broken English.

As irritated as I was with my host for abandoning me to his own pursuits, and as mad as I was at the pimps for engaging in their own pursuits at the peril of those young girls they were corrupting, I was really pissed off at myself for allowing this fiasco to unfold. Self-assertion has never been my strong point, as evidenced by a practiced inability to say NO to activities I would prefer to avoid. This was as good a time as any to firmly resolve to overcome my chronic weakness.

As the first hour gave way to the second, the crowd took on a shoulder to shoulder density. As my last nerve was ripe for plucking, my fickle host staggered down the carpeted stairway and slurred an alcohol and drug impaired, "Lezz-go."

For the second time in thirty minutes I grappled with the urge to do violence to a fellow human being. In lieu thereof, I grabbed his arm and helped him through the door half dragging, half pushing him the half block to the taxi pool area.

As we approached the waiting drivers they turned their backs to us in what seemed a choreographed move. My snarled, "I told you so," fell on his drug-deafened hearing as I reached for my wallet, and offered an advance payment of enough Vietnamese currency to repair the bridge burned earlier that afternoon.

****

At 5am the following morning I violently shook my host from his sleep. Once I was sure that he was uncomfortably conscious I thanked him for the "tour" and bid him goodbye. I could almost see the painful throb behind his unfocused eyes as he grabbed his head with both hands and uttered a mumbled, "Huh?" I enjoyed a moment of vengeful satisfaction in his misery then headed for breakfast.

By 9am I had completed my mission and, with signed documents in hand, walked to the airbase terminal. I had experienced enough of Saigon to last me a lifetime, and was anxious to return to the comparatively quiet suburban life of Vung Tau. Unfortunately, my SNAFU was to take another turn for the worse. SNAFU #3

I entered the terminal and eventually found the Information/Flight Assignment desk, currently occupied by a young Corporal with a facial expression that betrayed his authority complex. Noting his haughty demeanor I asked in my most pleasant, disarming tone, "Hi, could I get the next flight to Vung Tau?"

In an authoritative tone that matched his countenance he barked, "I need to see your orders, Specialist!"

"I don't have orders. I just hopped a flight yesterday from

Vung Tau."

"You can't fly anywhere in the Republic of Vietnam without orders!"

"Since, when?"

With a condescending sneer he announced, "Since 0600 hours this morning... Specialist." I'm sure he wanted to impress upon me that, even though I was a pay-grade higher than his rank of Corporal, he was in charge, and was claiming the high ground in administration of current policy.

Our short conversation continued during which I expressed my irritation with the Army's fickle propensity to alter policies and procedures on a whim, and he expressed that he didn't give a damn. My short exposure to the rude execution of his duties confirmed what I had always thought: A suitability test should be administered before authority, on any level, is granted to a peon with an attitude!

Overhearing the increasingly heated exchange, a soft spoken Master Sergeant stepped up beside me and in a deep, disarming southern tone said, "Son, I'm caught up in the same SNAFU. I'm catching a ride with some Aussies to Da Nang. Maybe they'll have a flight going your direction." Then with a chuckle he added, "If they have room, they'll take you along... if you have the nerve to fly with 'em!" While I appreciated his kindness, his humor didn't engender confidence in my only option to get back to Vung Tau!

The Australian troops were a hardy lot. Most American soldiers I knew simply tolerated their duty in Viet Nam. The Aussies seemed to enjoy, even thrive in it. They exuded a devil-may-care attitude that was catching. In my experience they were fun to be around and improved my attitude, even on bad days.

As the Master Sergeant and I neared a Caribou parked just off the edge of one of several runways, a grease streaked Aussie wearing a bush-hat, knee length shorts, combat boots and holding a wrench in each hand emerged from the open loading ramp of the airplane with a welcoming smile and a "G'dye, mites."

We explained our individual predicaments to our new "mite" and he directed the Master Sergeant to a temporary structure thirty yards away and instructed me to stay put. Before long he returned with the news that ten of his countrymen had arrived from the Mother country that morning, and were waiting for a flight to Vung Tau. My luck seemed to be changing!

An hour later, along with ten Aussie comrades, a pilot and a copilot, I boarded the very Caribou that my "mite" had been working on. The discouraging thing was that he was still tinkering with it.

The Caribou is entered from the back via a loading ramp that closes to become the back of the fuselage. Instead of a bench type seating arrangement, as in the C-123, a series of hammock like nets were suspended from the ceiling and walls of the aircraft, along with the familiar rope with a carabiner.

As we taxied into position for takeoff, I noticed that the ramp was still down which didn't concern me too much as my "mite" was still making what I assumed were final adjustments. At this point he was sitting on the hinged ramp with his legs dangling. When we came to a dead stop at the end of the runway and simply sat there, I became concerned that we weren't going anywhere. I could only assume that another SNAFU was about to occur in the form of mechanical difficulty. That concern was replaced with another as the engines came to full throttle and we moved forward, increasing our speed every second…with the ramp still wide open! My "mite" crawled forward grasping the closest dangling rope, and swung up into the one remaining net as the Caribou lifted off the tarmac!

Trying not to show panic I shouted at him over the roar of the engines, "Hey, shouldn't we tell the pilot the ramp is down?!"

He shouted back, "'ell, Mite, the damn thing's broke. She's been broke for a week. That's wha' I been tryin' t' fix!"

Through the gaping hole to my immediate left, I watched the tarmac become smaller and smaller as we soared at an uncomfortably steep angle, to get out of range of any opportunistic rifle fire from the lush green jungle below. I glanced at my "mite" who was now seated opposite me in the net, closest to the opening. He rested his right boot heel half in, half out of the plane, leaned back, tipped his hat over his eyes and prepared for a nap! I shuddered and closed my eyes.

Sixty air miles later we touched down on the Vung Tau airstrip and I bid my new "mites" goodbye. As I walked to the edge of the hot tarmac one of the Aussies caught up with me and asked, "'ows the sex 'ereabouts, mite."

I cautioned him, "I hear it's infected… and very risky."

He laughed and responded, "Aoin't it the truth…loife's full 'o risks."

This SNAFU had ended, but as sure as rain pours down in the monsoon season, another will soon occur to screw up an otherwise "g'dye."

****

To my pleasant surprise, I was about to find that not all SNAFUs are bad…

CHAPTER THIRTY-THREE

For whatever reason, I was experiencing a mild epidemic of pay vouchers being processed through my work station, devoid of the required validating signatures. The problem might have stemmed from my attempt to process payday transactions faster than usual, and with less double checking, in the interest of keeping the endless lines of anxious enlisted men moving and happy on their favorite day of the month.

Or perhaps it was due to the anxiety caused by the presumed need to simultaneously placate the occasional officer who refused to wait in line. Many were in the habit of visiting the commander's office upon arrival, usually on the pretense of making a social call, but in reality to request, or demand, special treatment and a personal escort to the back of my "cage". Others, expecting priority treatment, pulled rank and simply walked past the "Restricted" sign, banged on my back entrance, and shoved their vouchers through the bars. Distracted, I had to direct my attention to the disturbance behind me while the mob of waiting soldiers standing in front of my counter grew more antagonistic as they looked on in agitated disbelief. Although rhetorical, the most frequent question posed from the more anxious members in the long waiting line was, "Are you shittin' me?"

While multitasking may be expedient, distraction is the mother of oversight. The reason for the missing signatures didn't really matter; rectifying the error did! If the service member who failed to sign his pay voucher was stationed on base, the solution was simple; have him stop back and sign. It was more complicated if he or she were here on temporary duty and had returned to their home base. The latter of which was the most current case. Both Murphy's Law and the fundamentals of a classic SNAFU scenario were about to play out.

During the auditing of daily transactions on the day after payday, a voucher was discovered that didn't bare the signature of the recipient. To make matters worse, in accordance with the above fundamentals, the recipient had returned to his base camp which was located west of Can Tho, Vietnam, 130 air miles from our base at Vung Tau.

****

The commander appeared in front of my cage with the offending voucher in his hand, placed it on the counter and asked, "How would you like to take a chopper ride to Can Tho?"

"Isn't that located on the other side of the Mekong Delta?" I asked.

"Yes." He responded.

"Do I have a choice?"

"No."

Then he followed with, "I've ordered a chopper for tomorrow morning at 0830 hrs.

"Thank you, Sir, I'll be ready."

Then he added, "I don't anticipate any trouble, but take your sidearm."

I was going to carry it anyway, but I would have felt better if he hadn't thought it necessary!

****

Nocturnal daydreams. Together the terms form an oxymoron, but that night they filled my mind in place of dreams, which require sleep, which I didn't. One scenario after another paraded through my mind, some pleasant, some foreboding.

On the one hand, I hadn't had the opportunity to ride in a chopper, and that would probably be cool. The Vietnamese landscape is lush and beautiful from the air, and choppers don't fly too high, which should be beneficial to sightseeing, not to mention, my acrophobia would be less of an issue.

On the other hand, choppers don't fly too high, which could provide a slow moving target for an opportunistic enemy rifleman hiding in the lush landscape below.

My daydreaming continued. What was with these military desk jockey's and their obsession with signatures anyway? Was it really that important to send me hopping across Vietnam's landscape to obtain the signature of a fellow GI - a Corporal Johnson, who had simply forgotten to sign the voucher for his monthly gross income which totaled $205.00, including $90.00 combat pay?

The rumination continued off and on until dawn. I walked to the office as usual, retrieved my .45 from under my shirt, shoved it in my holster and buckled my pistol belt. Picking up the incomplete voucher, I headed for the commander's office and announced that I was leaving for the airfield; it was not so much a social amenity as it was to provide him with an opportunity to change his mind.

He didn't, and I began my trek to the airfield. As I walked outside the building I ran face first into a Corporal who was coming in the same door.

He asked, "Can you tell me where to find Specialist Schaar?"

With a whole bunch of happiness, I pointed to my name tag and said, "That's me, and I see by your name tag that you are Corporal Johnson."

Exchanging a smile, I handed him the voucher and pen. We had a short conversation, and marveled at the timing of the coincidence. He was coming back for another week of temporary duty at Vung Tau. Had I taken the chopper, it would have been just another run-of-the-mill SNAFU.

I walked back into the Commander's office, saluted and said with a smile, "Mission accomplished, Sir." Then I explained.

CHAPTER THIRTY-FOUR

The warm wind, blowing through my hair, provided a pleasant contrast to the breezeless stagnation offered by the prevailing atmosphere of our usual digs located a mile inland from the ocean. The gentle breeze wafting across Vung Tau Bay was augmented by the movement of our "Mike" boat heading into the wind at thirteen miles per hour. For the third time, the sporadic gusts had whipped the olive drab baseball cap from my head and sent it scooting across the deck. Tiring of the playful exchange with the elements I stuffed the cap securely into my pistol belt.

It was our first experience at exchanging US Dollars for Military Payment Certificates (MPC) for nearly 2,500 soldiers and Marines on an incoming troop ship. Our purpose was to convert all dollars on board the ship to MPCs before anyone disembarked. All US Currency would then be flown to Saigon for return to the states, thereby preventing circulation on the very active black market.

As our landing craft neared the anchored ship, I wondered how my party of three was going to board the vessel which appeared to become taller as we drew closer. My question was answered as we came along side and a narrow hatch on the side of the ship, about twenty-five feet above our boat, swung open and an even narrower rope ladder was thrown down to our deck!

The three of us were each laden with an eleven pound, loaded M-14 rifle slung over a shoulder, and a satchel full of documents. In addition to my rifle, I wore a pistol and carried a laundry bag containing about $70,000 dollars in MPCs. I questioned the need for all the firepower, but never received an answer. I always found it was more expedient to do what I was told…within reason.

An unencumbered ascent up the twenty feet of flopping rope ladder would have presented enough of a challenge in calm waters, but with our landing craft rising and falling five or so feet with every gentle wave, then banging into the side of the ship like two NFL players doing chest bumps, it seemed a daunting task.

Aside from the obvious physical challenge of climbing from the boat to the hatch with my awkward load in tow, that dangling, dancing rope ladder summoned from the depths of my psyche an all too familiar phobia.

As it applied to my personal mental makeup, acrophobia was not limited to the fear of standing atop tall structures, or peering over the edge of cliffs, or even flying in an aircraft. Ladders, let alone flexible ladders, held their own special horror! In addition to my small repertoire of unfounded fears I could see the potential for a number of lethal scenarios including falling overboard, drowning, being smooshed between the two bouncing watercraft, or a combination of all three – not necessarily in any particular order!

I glanced at the expectant faces of my two assistants and resolved that I would not allow myself to be embarrassed by that phobic "monkey on my back." With no further delay, I wound the drawstring of the laundry bag over the barrel of my rifle, acquired a death grip on the ladder and awkwardly climbed to the open hatch.

A Naval Officer leaned out of the hatch and grabbed the laundry bag as a sailor standing beside him reached for my hand and pulled me in – well actually only half way in, because my rifle barrel snagged the top of the hatch and held me there for a tense moment.

We had come prepared to spend most of the day exchanging currency, but to our surprise, the Naval Finance Officer (the Purser) had collected all the cash in advance of our arrival and had all the necessary forms signed. I transferred the legal tender to my laundry bag and carefully descended the ladder to my two waiting comrades who hadn't left the deck of the landing craft.

We learned a lot from our first nautical currency exchange: Satchels stuffed with 2,500 authorizations were not needed, I didn't need my two assistants and we did not need all that firepower. Most important to me, I learned that I could force myself to overcome my phobias, at least in a limited fashion. I'm still plagued with acrophobia, but it only kicks in at heights above twenty-five vertical feet.

The procedural lessons we learned were of limited use as we only had two more exchanges before the use of troop ships was deemed too slow for the growing need for manpower in the prosecution of the escalating war. The task of bringing soldiers and Marines to Vietnam was turned over to the Military Air Transport Service, allowing for a faster and more efficient influx of boots on the ground.

"MIKE" boat on the Mekong Delta

CHAPTER THIRTY-FIVE

In mid-1960s Vietnam there were no cell phones, and international telephone usage was restricted to military transmissions.

Although frustratingly slow, the U.S. Postal Service provided the only line of communication with the people, places and lives that we loved. Precious letters made up the largest percentage of our mail, but the occasional package from home arriving at "mail call" held a special thrill.

Not being one to wait for a special occasion or holiday, Mom kept my comrades and me supplied with copies of the hometown newspaper, cookies and assorted treats every week or so. My favorites – chocolate chip – were referred to by my hootch mates as chocolate spots, since exposure to the tropical heat melted the chips into tiny chocolate puddles that permeated the cookies. Regardless of their structural integrity, or lack thereof, I've never eaten a chocolate chip cookie I didn't love.

A week before Christmas Day 1966 I received a box from my sister containing a twelve inch tall Christmas tree complete with battery powered blinking lights and an over-spray of a granulated sugary substance representing snow. The accompanying note said, "I didn't want you to have another Christmas without a tree."

On Christmas Eve we placed the thoughtful gift on my footlocker and turned on the blinking lights. I fell asleep watching the multicolored hues reflecting off the walls and ceiling of my cubicle. The soft light brought a warm glow to the room as well as to me.

Awakening at dawn I was surprised to see the lights still twinkling merrily, albeit on the wires and skeletal remains of our tree. Obviously we had been visited during the wee hours of Christmas morning, not by reindeer, but rats. Drawn by the sugary coating (which was actual sugar), they had chewed their way into the hootch and, undeterred by the blinking lights, dined on the edible portion of the tree.

****

Acts of thoughtfulness weren't limited only to family members…

It was an exceptionally sticky afternoon even for Southeast Asia, when a rectangular shaped package arrived for me at mail call. My day was made as I recognized the name and return address of a kind lady I had known since childhood. She hailed from West Virginia, and it was indeed a good day for us when she left those beautiful hills and became part of our lives. A faithful member of my home church, she was always the first to show up at fund raisers with a variety of tasty treats to donate to whatever current cause needed support.

I told my hovering comrades they were in for a special treat as I slowly opened the carefully sealed package. Peeling off the several layers of plastic wrap revealed a cake… or bread…or something…covered with a vivid blue-green topping.

An audible wave of let-down swept through the small gathering as we realized that the colorful "icing" was actually a well-developed mold that would have brought tears of joy to the eyes of Alexander Fleming. Light hearted anticipation wilted as the musty odor of mold wafted through the humid air of the hootch sending the dejected group back to their respective areas without dessert.

My disappointment over the spoiled offering faded as I thought again of the sweet lady who had gone to a lot of work to make my day brighter, and realized that she had actually succeeded. The old adage, "It's the thought that counts," was perfectly defined by this moment.

Hesitating briefly, I reluctantly tossed the ill-fated cake or banana bread or whatever it was into the trash then sat down to write a note thanking her for her kindness. I told her how delicious it was and how much we enjoyed it, without specifics as to what it might have been. It has always been proper to bend the truth in letters from a war zone; it makes everyone feel better and lessens the concern and worry of the folks back home.

The gift had accomplished the giver's purpose in that her kindness had transcended the negative effects of the heat, the mold and the limitations of the Postal Service. Her intention was to let me know I was in her thoughts, not merely to give me something to munch on.

I finished the letter and headed for the mess hall with a renewed spring in my step, even though I knew the chow I was about to eat would taste, as usual, like it had been cooked in Clorox.

CHAPTER THIRTY-SIX

*"Absence is to love as wind is to fire;
it extinguishes the small, it enkindles the great."*
Roger de Bussy-Rabutin Circa AD 1660

History tells us that Roger Rabutin was involved with several wars as well as several women, so I'm going to assume that he knew what he was talking about.

All wars have exacted a heavy toll on lives, limbs and sanity as well as personal relationships, marriages and fidelity.

During our first day of basic training a mean spirited training sergeant told us to get thoughts of home and women out of our heads, because if we didn't pay attention to our training, we probably wouldn't make it back there anyway. As if that hadn't grabbed our attention, he added that we should forget that "pretty little gal" we left there, because she was being taken care of by some other local stud who was too smart to enlist and crafty enough to avoid the draft.

He ended his dispiriting tirade with, "They're probably already shacked up, so get her outta your head and pay attention to me! I'm gonna show you how to stay alive when some asshole is trying to make you dead!"

I knew that his verbal harassment was a necessary part of the psychological battering that we had to prove we could endure. Sadly, in many cases, his disturbing scenario wasn't far from reality.

****

About six months into our tour of Vietnam a young GI from a small mid-west farm community joined our team. When his National Guard unit had been called to active duty, his Military Occupational Status listed him as a driver. Due to a fairly common SNAFU he wound up in our Finance Detachment rather than the Motor Pool.

A soft spoken country boy, he had down home values, but no street smarts. He just wanted to get his military commitment behind him and return to the rural life and the girl he loved. Like many other soldiers in past wars, as well as this one, he had a steady girlfriend and when called to active duty thought the best course of action was to marry her and stake his claim. The nuptials were hurriedly arranged and they embarked on two weeks of church and state sanctioned bliss before his deployment.

Now he was in steamy Southeast Asia, experiencing separation anxiety, depression and several other negative emotions that were included with the tour package.

It was one month to the day since his arrival in-country when he received the dreaded letter from his new bride asking for a divorce or annulment or whatever he could afford! She had found someone who made her "feel special" and didn't want to be tied down anymore.

Adding what she apparently thought constituted solid reasoning in support of her request was the line that tore his heart out; "What if something happens to you over there and you don't come home? What am I supposed to do?" His fickle young wife's letter glowed with a self-centered immaturity that equaled his disastrous notion that a marriage contract could secure her love.

His bunk mate saw the letter drop from his quivering hand and asked if he was ok. There was no answer – just a blank stare. After reading the letter, the bunk mate passed it to a small group gathered around. We tried to console him, but he was unapproachable and just sat silent.

Some of the hootch mates conspired, on his behalf, to take him downtown, get him drunk and get him a hooker. I suggested that adding exposure to gonorrhea, syphilis, and a host of other venereal diseases to his depression might not be the best action plan. He wanted none of it anyway. His bunkmate brought a couple beers to share, and his mood seemed to improve with each can he consumed. As more of us joined the impromptu therapy session, he actually laughed and joked with his circle of supportive friends. He eventually fell asleep; half drunk, but asleep. We congratulated ourselves on bringing him through his crisis, or so we thought...

Next day at the office was drudgery for him. At quitting time he was the first to suggest going for a few beers. We welcomed his new attitude as a sign of recovery and joined him for more than a few.

He seemed to find a degree of relief in drinking with a crowd each night. As the booze worked its magic, he went willingly along for the effervescent ride then crashed into a solemn state and talked of suicide. When this happened, whoever was with him, and sober enough, would try to encourage him with lines like, "Aw c'mon man, don't talk like that. No woman is worth that. You'll find another one," and on and on.

It soon became obvious to everyone but him that he was developing an unquenchable appetite for pity as well as booze. I don't think he ever seriously contemplated suicide, but as his daily entourage became less sympathetic and began to dwindle, his intake of alcohol increased with or without company. Large quantities of beer were soon superseded by smaller but stronger portions of hard liquor.

He regularly maxed out his Class Six Card. (The government subsidized allowance of six bottles of hard liquor per month, at extremely reduced cost to service members.) Regardless of his intake of alcohol each evening, he always showed up for work next morning with the rest of us. I couldn't help feeling sorry for him, but he wouldn't accept help or advice and continued to crawl into a bottle at every opportunity. I never heard from him after Vietnam and don't know if he ever regained his grip on life. I hope he did.

****

In military usage "collateral damage" is the term that describes the unintended destruction of life or property resulting from a combat action. In a broader sense, the term could describe the unintended damage to the personal relationships of service members, separated from their families, while serving in a combat zone. In either case the damage can be devastating to the unintended victim.

CHAPTER THIRTY-SEVEN

The last two months of my tour were passing slowly and without incident. I reminded myself repeatedly that my nemesis, the interim officer, had been transferred elsewhere and I could relax and enjoy the best parts of my tropical surroundings without concern.

Unconvinced by my own reasoning I remained in a mental state of consternation and readiness. A nagging concern bordering on distraction, if not paranoia, continued to control my idle time thoughts to the extent that the idea of being more than grasping distance from my weapon was out of the question.

****

Like many of my fellow soldiers I made a daily ritual of crossing each passing day from the calendar, plodding slowly with a pencil toward my DEROS. (Date Estimated Return from Overseas) That day finally arrived in August 1967.

With paperwork complete, orders in hand and my flight to Tan Son Nhut confirmed I began the round of obligatory goodbyes. At the end of the work day, whether by force of habit or lingering apprehension, I stuffed my pistol in the waistband of my fatigues and walked to the hootch for the last time. All that stood between me and my flight were nine hours of darkness.

With my duffle bag packed full of all my government issued possessions, and fully dressed in a uniform appropriate for travel, I laid awake on my bunk with thoughts of home while wishing the night away. Then like a bad dream I began mulling over the death of an extended family member that had occurred at the very end of World War II…

With the dangerous part of the war behind him he had just

arrived at a base in England and was preparing his combat gear for turn-in. A fellow soldier in the next bunk was deep in conversation with him about their impending return home. His bunk mate was distractedly cleaning his M-1 rifle for the last time while discussing his after the war plans. A forgotten round in the rifle's chamber accidentally detonated, sending its bullet through the head of my distant cousin whom I never had the pleasure of meeting.

With that disturbing bit of family history invading my thoughts and the anticipation of leaving Vietnam at daylight, sleep was not an option. At 3am, I simply had to make my move, but I had one last thing to do…

I quietly awakened one of my trusted friends, a somewhat reluctant soldier from a wealthy family in Cincinnati and told him I needed a favor.

Groggy, but civil considering the hour, he responded, "Sure, what do you need?"

I cleared the chamber of my pistol and handed it to him as I asked, "Can you put this back in my cage tomorrow?"

I responded to his questioning look with, "Don't ask, just do it for me."

Stuffing it under his pillow he said, "Sure, why not?"

Then he added, with a handshake, "See ya stateside."

"Roger that, and thank you."

With that, I grabbed my duffle bag and walked to the airstrip guided by the occasional security light. Arriving at the tarmac, I climbed atop a Conex container, leaned back against my bag and waited, wide awake, the remaining five hours until my flight.

****

Processing out of the Army is pretty much like processing in, only backwards. You stand in one of many lines for the same physical examinations, and when instructed to do so, bend over in unison as a faceless medic shines a bright light on each row of exposed butts.

As we approached the final station, a sergeant announced the only deviation from the expected routine. He barked, "Anyone present who has been wounded, injured or hospitalized for more than twenty-four hours while in-country, form a line on the left." Several, myself included, stepped to the left.

Turning his attention to the newly formed line he continued, "You men have extra paperwork to complete and further medical exams that should take another two days during which time you will be barracked here at th...

I heard nothing he said after, "another two days", and with the thought of more poking and prodding and bureaucratic paperwork looming before me, I once again took matters into my own hands. No way was I going to spend one more day, let alone two, "in-country" for any reason.

This was a SNAFU that I could fix myself! As the group on the right was ordered to move to the final station, I side stepped and quietly slipped back into their ranks and marched with them.

****

Two hours later, a kind stewardess welcomed us aboard our "Freedom Bird". I'm sure she had greeted thousands of GI faces on countless flights to and from the states, but she still sported her best majorette smile for each of us as we stepped onto her plane.

The first leg of the flight to Toccata, Japan was surprisingly quick, and our time on the ground was of short duration. We re-boarded within the hour for the long flight to Anchorage, Alaska. All sense of time was lost as we crossed one time zone after another on our flight over the Pacific. Nodding in and out of sleep from one long hour to the next contributed to the jet lag experience.

Our flight touched down at Anchorage International Airport at 5am Alaska time on whatever day it was. We got off the plane and dined sumptuously on a breakfast provided by any number of vending machines located in the concourse of the then tiny airport. Benjamin Franklin's assertion that, "hunger is the best pickle," could not have seemed more profound as I dined on the best tasting cheese and peanut butter crackers I had ever tasted.

"Freedom Bird" flight home

I can't quite explain the feeling of exhilaration that swept over my shivering body as I stepped back onto the cold tarmac and strolled toward our waiting plane. It was mid-August but the early morning air was cold, crisp, fresh and most assuredly American. I took a deep breath and had that reassuring feeling that, if the need arose, I would have no trouble walking the rest of the way home on my own two feet – I was stateside!

The need did not arise. The jet engines started, and we began our high altitude trek across the Canadian wilderness to McGuire Air Force Base, New Jersey. The duration of that flight taxed the butt-in-seat experience to a nearly intolerable level.

Happiness is an inadequate term to describe the euphoria of the moment I stepped off that plane at McGuire Air Force Base. I was happy and thankful to be alive, happy to be stateside and happy to be off the plane – God, I was happy! And I told Him so!

Another day of processing out at nearby Fort Dix, and I was unceremoniously released from active duty and free to go home.

Getting a military standby flight was very iffy, and being intolerant of any further delay, I hired a cab to the Philadelphia train station. Boarding the next west bound train, I road all night long as my chosen means of transportation made very slow progress across the darkened Pennsylvania landscape, stopping at nearly every town, village and burg along the way.

Arriving at the train station in Dennison, Ohio around 9am I descended the steel steps of the passenger car, still on an emotional high. I jumped from the last step onto the same spot on the platform where I had boarded a similar west bound train fifteen months before at the lowest emotional ebb of my life.

A few minutes later I was vigorously hugging and kissing the absolute love of my life, ready to begin the life that had been on hold for the past four years. My brother and sister came with her to meet me in his new 1967 VW Beetle. My duffle bag, my sweetheart and I squeezed into the tiny back seat for the ride home, oblivious to, and happy with, our cramped accommodations.

Dennison Depot, Dennison, Ohio

CHAPTER THIRTY-EIGHT

Return to civilian life was unexpectedly awkward, perhaps due to my skewed expectations of coming home to a comparative heaven after witnessing some of the bad stuff and unpleasant living conditions found in the broader world outside the borders of our blessed country. Naïvely, I had anticipated returning to the same environment I had left three years before. When I left, politics had seemed simple and bordered on the humdrum. Everyone had an opinion on everything, but in most cases, unless their issue was of burning urgency, kept their opinions to themselves.

Perhaps part of the awkwardness was due to the diverse mixture of attitudes and opinions regarding the war. As strange as it may seem, I hadn't formed a solid position on my Vietnam experience – politically or philosophically. Maybe I was too busy performing my assigned duties to form an opinion as to the validity of, let alone the gradual month to month escalation that seemed to be the government's battle plan for prosecuting the war. My rank and duties didn't qualify me for a daily briefing on the progress or lack thereof of the struggle. The Army Times newspaper certainly didn't offer enough information to make me, or any other soldier with boots on the ground, an expert on our very own war. Had we been updated daily like the news-watching, armchair quarterbacks back home, I'm confident that opinions would have flowed as freely as American and Vietnamese blood in any one of many battles. Being too close to the daily action made it difficult for any of us to "see the forest for the trees."

Thank God I was from a small town, and was spared the sad, and sometimes violent, reception that greeted many of my fellow soldiers. I was welcomed back warmly by my friends, family and coworkers.

Exacerbating the awkwardness, the occasional casual acquaintance would pose an uncomfortable question regarding the war for which I, embarrassingly, had no answer.

From the immature crowd questions like, "How many guys did you kill?" Or from a few of the more politically astute, "How do you justify our country's involvement in this war?" What could I say? My head was still spinning from reentry into the "world," and I wasn't prepared for the pop quizzes.

****

Things happened fast during my first few months as a civilian:
Picking up the telephone for the first time in years, I found that our local system had grown at least three extra digits referred to as an area code. The second surprising advance in technology was the universal private line. It was no longer necessary to pick up the phone gingerly then listen to be sure no one else was on our party line.

In one of my first quiet moments alone I revisited my childhood playground, Muskrat Bottom, only to find that it had been sold to a local developer who apparently thought the fastest return on his investment would be to turn the once fertile farm land into the county's largest mobile home park. Construction was underway as I descended the old tractor path and watched as the rich, dark soil that once oozed through my toes was being buried under tons of concrete, asphalt and metal. Realizing that progress is sometimes a double-edged sword, I accepted the fate of my playground, and walked back up the tractor path for the last time. After all, people had to have an affordable place to live.

The surrounding landscape hadn't escaped change either. A new inter-state highway had been plopped down through corn fields and farms that had been vastly altered or were no longer there. Familiar roads that I had enjoyed cruising in my

'61 Chevy had been rerouted.

Speaking of my '61 Chevy – my beautiful car was gone. About eighteen months before my return I had asked Dad to sell it while it still had some value. It had already begun to develop a terminal case of rust from exposure to the salt and slush of our northeast Ohio winters.

I was only home a few days before returning to my job at the bank. Anxious to restart my life, I didn't want any time off. Getting back to work allowed less time for more questions and awkward moments. Compulsive unpleasant thoughts, memories and nightmares were not an issue as long as I was busy. Getting back to my bank job was therapeutic.

****

With the everyday stress of my Vietnam experience seeming to fade, I once again attempted to enjoy the amenities and safety of small town life. I reasoned that it was time to let my guard down, quit looking over my shoulder and sleep soundly at night. Unfortunately, I found that plan easier to imagine than to implement.

I had carried a weapon for most of the previous year and found it difficult to relax enough to go to sleep without being armed. This was before the days of licensed concealed carry, and I wasn't about to ignore local law by carrying a concealed weapon in public as I had done in Vietnam. Even with the immediate threat of a likely attack behind me, the uneasy feeling remained. I began comparing myself to an alcoholic or drug addict who had relied on an adopted crutch too long to be without it.

With a limited knowledge of psychology I began to assume that my obsession with security, both mine and those around me, might be symptomatic of a mild case of paranoia. Self-diagnosis is, more often than not, too subjective to be of value in treating maladies other than a headache or upset stomach. It was years later that I turned to professionals for an objective, not to mention correct, diagnosis.

In trying to discover the source of my compulsion to be constantly on guard, I reasoned that, because I was in charge of our living quarters in Vietnam, I had felt duty bound, to the point of obsession, to protect my hootch mates. With that in mind, why would I not do what was necessary to protect my family, and future family, from danger right here at home?

Maybe I was over thinking the probability of "danger at home", but my reasoning might have been skewed because I had seen some unhinged people do some unspeakable things during the last year. Rejecting the idea of getting sleeping pills which would make me even more useless as a defender, I decided to err on the side of caution and buy my own weapon. That plan became unnecessary due to a chance happening a few days later…

The President of my bank called me into his office and closed the door behind me. Noting the look on my face, he assured me with a chuckle, that I wasn't being fired and asked me to have a seat. I was surprised as he reached into his desk drawer and withdrew a Colt .38 Special revolver and laid it on his desk in front of me. As my eyes focused on the empty cylinder the immediate thought of being shot by my boss faded.

Unbeknownst to me and most other employees, the revolver was one of two that had been part of the bank's "security plan" since the 1930's. One was in the President's desk, the other in the drawer of the head teller.

A lengthy explanation followed regarding modern banking and insurance regulations. These he interpreted as discouraging the presence of weapons inside bank buildings as a potential liability that the insurance companies were unwilling to underwrite. He and the Chairman of the Board had decided that now was the time to quietly get rid of them. It was agreed that the Chairman would take one, and I would be offered the other as I was fresh out of the military and could probably handle a gun. I didn't agree or disagree with their logic. I just accepted the fortuitous presentation of the weapon and thanked him.

I had no intention of carrying my new weapon on me

during the day. The need for my crutch occurred at night when I found, once again, that sound sleep wasn't possible unless a gun was within reaching distance.

Over the next few weeks I made several trips to a nearby abandoned strip mine to become familiar with my new weapon. Although it was a bona fide antique, the gun hadn't been fired since it left the manufacturer. After my near fatal experience with the break in at Vung Tau, I vowed to never handle a weapon again unless I knew it inside and out!

Several hundred rounds later, I felt that I had achieved an adequate degree of proficiency to handle the weapon safely and effectively. The routine of placing the loaded weapon under my pillow, every night before turning in, became as mindless as any other repetitive task.

CHAPTER THIRTY-NINE

A short five months after my return from Vietnam while I was still living at home, my hard working, mild mannered, loving Dad, whom I had never spent enough time with, was killed in a horrible mining accident.

It was a cold, snowy January night in 1968. A blinding snow storm developed during his work shift and, true to his nature, he told his fellow workers to walk behind the dozer as he plowed a path back to their cars. According to the men with him, the wind and snow made seeing nearly impossible. The dozer went over the edge of a high-wall.

Dad died as he had lived – working hard and helping those around him. He was 60 years old. He was a wonderful man.

****

With Dad gone, I took on the task of providing emotional and physical support as well as offering my opinion regarding major decisions for my mother. In spite of a chronic lung problem, and a nagging emptiness from the loss of her beloved spouse, she kept up with her responsibilities as Office Manager for a local optometrist. Keeping busy with her job, family and church was how she coped with her physical limitations and loss of her companion.

Even with her physical constraints Mom was a go-getter and forged her own way in life, raising her family and working at office type jobs when possible to help with expenses. An example of her "forging ahead" was related to me recently by the doctor for whom she worked as Office Manager:

After completing eight consecutive years of college, the

young doctor had chosen, in spite of a locally glum business climate for a new optometry practice, to establish his business in New Philadelphia. He and his wife wanted to start a family in an environment similar to what they had enjoyed growing up here in Tuscarawas County. Their belief in the importance of raising a successful, happy family in the nurturing environment of a small town trumped the financial advantage of maximizing his income by locating his practice in a larger metropolitan area.

With an overwhelming, but necessary, investment in a building, technical equipment and inventory, he opened his practice in an area already saturated with several established optometry practices. He worked alone for the first two years, and projected that it would be five years before he could afford to hire help, but that changed...

In his words, "I got a phone call one morning at 9:00. It was a nice, kind voice. She said she had been working at an office supply store in downtown New Philadelphia, but wanted to change jobs, and asked if I needed help. (I hadn't said a word since I had answered the phone). She continued by saying she would be at my office at 8:00 tomorrow morning, ready to work. Good bye."

"Still holding the receiver, it took me about ten seconds to realize that someone had just called me, sight unseen, and hired herself!"

Together, the doctor and my mom built one of the best practices in Ohio. He described Mom as, "prim, proper, smart, compassionate, but firm if need be."

Over the next few years, she adopted her boss and his family as if he were another son, observing all special occasions and birthdays as she did those of her own family.

Mom always felt that her marriage to Dad was a match made in Heaven. I'm sure she felt that her blessed association with her doctor/boss originated at the same source.

****

Life is a mixed bag of sad events and happy times; if we're lucky, the mixture is heavy on happy. It was six months after Dad's death that I married the only girl I ever loved.

CHAPTER FORTY

We only wanted a small wedding. We had been separated for most of our courtship, and the formality of a large wedding seemed like just another frustrating delay.

When we felt the time was right, we checked with our minister and, at the risk of making it look like a "have to" situation, set the date for the following week. The minister, who always thought that bigger was better, took upon himself the task of announcing from the pulpit the very next Sunday that our "open church" wedding would be the following Saturday.

From our pew near the center of the church I turned to my soon to be bride and asked breathlessly, "What?"

Everything spun out of control from there. My very capable bride swung into action Monday morning lining up everything needed for a church wedding. Calls to out-of-state relatives were placed in lieu of written invitations, which would have been way too slow. Cake and ice cream were ordered for the reception. Best Man and Maid of Honor were drafted... and I went to work as usual!

It still amazes me that our wedding was put together in the ten day period prior to the ceremony at the end of a five year courtship. For the record, I can state truthfully, that there was no ulterior imperative for the rush, as confirmed ten months and one day after the wedding by the birth of our first beautiful daughter. Further confirmation came from a raft of busy bodies that were tallying the elapsed days of gestation! Thus is life in a small town!

****

Our wedding day dawned on a hot July Saturday. At the time I worked for a less than gracious boss, who couldn't see the logic in giving me the morning off, as the wedding wasn't scheduled until 7pm that evening. As it turned out, I was the last employee to leave work that day! What a guy.

Adding to the already tense schedule, the minister was scheduled to be out of town for part of the week of the wedding, but felt it necessary to put a new coat of paint on the social hall prior to the reception - a task he assigned to his two reluctant teenage sons. Never one to panic, he assured us that it would be ready in plenty of time. In his absence, the painting hadn't commenced until Friday. The final coat was applied on Saturday morning – just seven hours prior to the music starting!

Our small "family only" wedding turned out to be a wall buster, with the little church packed to the doors! With the exception of parroting the words cued by the minister, gazing into the beautiful green eyes of my smiling red haired bride, and realizing that we were finally where we wanted to be, the details of the ceremony are a complete blank. I do, however, recall the smell of drying paint adding its chemical bouquet to that of the floral arrangements as we entered the reception hall!

My new father-in-law, who was never at a loss for ideas or words, had hired an acquaintance, a shutterbug hobbyist, to photograph the proceedings, because he "had a new camera." Prior to the digital era, film needed developed so it was a week later when we saw the results of the photographer's sincere, but amateur efforts.

Explaining to us why he had photographed the wedding cake from the backside instead of the ornamented front, he said the light coming through the window just didn't illuminate the front of the cake!

As the evening of greeting, thanking and socializing neared its merciful conclusion, my new father–in-law took charge again and invited all who were interested to come to our new tiny rental in the country to watch us open our gifts! Needless to say, all were interested!

We, along with our entourage of interested people, left the bulging church building to cram into our smaller house which also bulged. Many of the men graciously volunteered to relieve the crowding by milling around outside and doing whatever men do when escaping uncomfortable, not to mention hot, social occasions.

It seemed as though they were never going to leave, so shortly after 11pm, I remembered that we had just filled our freezer with many, individually wrapped, ice cream squares left over from the reception. Desperately wanting our friends to leave, I removed the frozen squares from the freezer, placing several each in plastic bags and began handing them out to the men outside, asking them to take the bars home as we would never use them all. The plan worked like a charm, as the ice cream toting husbands hurried to their respective wives and ushered them to their waiting cars as the frozen favors began to melt.

Relief sometimes comes with tears. As the last carload of friends and family drove away from our tiny home, I turned to comfort my teary eyed bride. With our long separation, and the long tense day of matrimonial formalities behind us, the sudden quietness of the moment was overwhelming. Our wedding evening hadn't played out the way I had imagined, but it was the beginning of the most blessed union of a man and a woman imaginable.

That night wasn't the end of all our problems, but I knew there would be nothing come our way that we couldn't handle, because we were finally together.

****

We talked and hugged into the wee hours of the morning until the stress and hubbub of our wedding day began to fade. Exhausted, my bride and I gave in to the need for sleep.

It was eerily quiet in our new home. The only sound was her soft breathing. A mild adrenaline rush swept over me as I considered the new journey we had just begun. I had a new purpose in life, a new responsibility and a precious friend to love and protect.

As I lay back, I felt the familiar reassuring lump of my .38 revolver under the pillow.

The next morning my bride of twelve hours kissed me, then gazed distractedly beside my head and asked, "What's that?"

My revolver had migrated from its resting place and the barrel was protruding from beneath the pillow. It was then that I learned the importance of sharing pertinent information with one's spouse. I was also introduced, for the first time, to the concept of joint decision making.

After a few short moments of negotiation, punctuated with peck like kisses and gentle hugging, I agreed to keep my weapon in the drawer of the night stand, where it remained for the next fifty-odd years.

My beautiful bride Carol and me

****

That was probably the first time that my "problem" was noticed by anyone other than me. At that time, references to post-traumatic stress disorder (PTSD) were seldom made. Occasionally, the subject would come up, but the malady didn't seem to apply to me and eventually found its way to my mental back burner.

****

There was no time for a honeymoon. The Monday morning following the wedding I returned to work, life went into high gear and maintained its momentum until my retirement forty-one years later. The continuing inability to say NO contributed to an already busy life style by adding an uncomfortable level of volunteer activity to my daily comings and goings. While I understand the intent of the quaint saying, "Busy fingers are happy fingers", there are limits! Let me explain...

CHAPTER FORTY-ONE

As Mom's health declined, my job of advisor expanded into caregiver. Taking prescribed medication to ease her breathing aggravated other health issues and her already compromised ability to function on her own began a downward spiral.

She did what she could to deal with a condition that became increasingly emotionally distressing. Filling her days with inspirational readings, and speaking with faithful friends by phone kept her reasonably content, but her happiness was never complete because she never allowed herself to get over losing Dad.

The old axiom, "Time heals all wounds" applies in many cases, but Mom grieved the loss of my dad until the day she died at 72.

****

Prior to Mom's death, while I was still assisting her daily, I received a call from an aunt, who was close to ninety years old, asking me to stop over to help her with a problem. She had no children and I had helped her before with minor repairs to both car and home on several occasions.

She was a dear lady who had opinions – nay convictions - that she didn't mind sharing with interested and non-interested parties alike. She marched to her own drummer through each day, beginning every morning with a generous application of cherry red rouge, in quarter sized circles, on each powered cheek. On days when she would be out and about, she added a brilliant, but matching, shade of lipstick. With her daily toilette complete, she adorned the bodice of her ever present apron with tiny hand written notes listing her intended projects for the day, pinning them upside down for easy access and reading.

She was very community minded and, having no children of her own, enjoyed providing assistance to children's groups in any way she could. She loved acquiring used dolls at thrift stores and yard sales. Painting on new faces and dressing them in appropriately sized clothing of her own design, she donated hundreds over the years for distribution by local organizations to needy families at Christmas time.

Interestingly enough, she lived in the mobile home park situated on what used to be my playground, Muskrat Bottom. As I neared the entrance to her allotment later that day, I noticed the familiar signs on either side of the entrance had crumbled into disheveled heaps of brick. When she greeted me at her front door I asked, "What in the world happened to the signs?"

With a sheepish grin she said, "That's what I wanted to talk with you about."

She had driven to the local grocery that morning and wrecked into the exit sign on her way out of her street. Then, upon her return, took out the entrance sign with the same fender! She wanted to talk with me about where to take her car for the body work!

It was obvious that she was in need of closer supervision. Thus began a daily trek across town to check on my dear aunt during my lunch hour, which soon became an hour to do anything but lunch. Conveniently, I was Manager of the bank's main office by then, so no one questioned the extra ten minutes I tacked onto that hour…at least, not to my face. As her mental faculties waned and she needed more frequent assistance, my unofficial caregiver status became official.

During one of the more memorable "lunch hour" visits I discovered what appeared to be a poor attempt at abstract art with a Tuscan texture on her kitchen ceiling. She explained that she had been heating a can of condensed milk, sat down to rest and totally forgot about it until the explosion wakened her.

Several consecutive lunch hours plus a paint splotched dress shirt and necktie later, the repainting was complete.

Prior to my aunt's passing at 93, I was asked by an aging uncle, who lived nearby, if I could stop by his home on my way to work each morning, and help him get his orthopedic stocking on. His logic seemed unassailable –it was on my way to work and should only take a few minutes!

Individually, my efforts to provide assistance as needed to everyone in need would have made for a hectic schedule, but combined with keeping my family, my employer, my church, my service club, my fellow members on several boards and my friends happy, is it any wonder that I was the only banker in the county who didn't take up golf?

CHAPTER FORTY-TWO

So, what exactly was my "problem" referred to earlier in these pages?

With regard to emotional stability I'm a happy, even tempered person. Daily irritations or negative situations that might send my fellow human beings into an emotional tail spin are of little or no consequence to my peace of mind. Conversely, especially in later life, I have experienced increased emotional sensitivity to events, and even thoughts that would probably cause no concern or reaction in others.

Post-Traumatic Stress Disorder (PTSD) can spring from any number of distressful situations, and manifests symptoms in varying degrees at different times throughout the lifetime of the victim. The symptoms may appear early after a causative occurrence or take years to become observable. A busy, involved lifestyle may keep the symptoms at bay so they do not become evident even to the sufferer.

During my years of employment with the bank, I looked forward to my annual two week mandatory vacation with a mild dread. My young family looked forward to vacation time with excitement, and was happy to be a part of whatever we decided to do or wherever we went. So I put on my happy face for their benefit, gritted my teeth in private, and off we went to a nearby theme park or a not too distant lake or, on rare occasions, the nearest ocean; a crazy way to enjoy a family vacation, huh?

My reluctance to be away from home and job was based in the uncomfortable feeling caused by leaving, even for a short time, the people who depended on me each day – my semi-invalid mom, my aging aunt, my needy uncle, not to mention the clients and employees in my charge.

That was stressful enough, but the icing on my agitated mental cake was that the suspension of daily responsibilities provided ample time to dredge up thoughts and memories, both current and, even more disturbing, distant. Memories flowed uninvited of actions I could have taken, but didn't, things I shouldn't have done, but did. Ultimately, my thoughts cycled to disturbing scenes and events I was witness to, or part of, in Vietnam; many of which I have chosen to exclude from these pages. Nightmares disturbed my fitful sleep.

When I returned from vacation to the hectic normalcy of my life, the compulsive mental rehash of events was forced to that crowded back burner and the nightmares, to some extent, subsided.

****

Eventually, my long awaited retirement date came and the daily grind was suddenly put behind me. The first few months of retirement were glorious and filled with promise. Then the freedom of finally being able to plan and do things without a tight schedule, once again allowed too much down time.

Horrible dreams once again became the nightly norm; their subject matter vacillating between disturbing scenarios, and hideous interactive scenes that would have made an academy award quality horror movie. Acting out the more violent dreams became a danger to my sleeping wife. Sometimes I tried to stay awake, thinking that if I was exhausted enough I wouldn't dream. That didn't work. For safety sake I relocated my firearm from the night stand to our bedroom closet, where I would have to be alert, or at least awake, to access it.

Finally, at the urging of another Vietnam veteran and my loving wife, I agreed to talk with a Veterans Administration psychologist – It was the best move I had made thus far to address my problem.

The entire experience was cathartic. I felt I could unload every thought and particle of constipated emotion that I had carried for years, because she said she wanted to hear it, and assured me that she wouldn't be shocked at anything I told her.

I had always kept my problems to myself. My wife and I have always been open and shared concerns and vital information equally, but I didn't want to burden her with a problem that I didn't think we could solve anyway. On the rare occasion that emotion gained control and a tear escaped, and she would ask what was wrong, I would brush it off and changed the subject.

I felt a different bond with my psychologist and case worker. There was no need to protect them from my demons, and every reason to finally share them. Maybe keeping my problems private is in my DNA. I never heard my dad complain about anything, with the possible exception of rotten politicians. He worked quietly, helped others when needed and, if he ever had a pain or problem, he was the only one aware of it.

Several therapy sessions later I felt that my emotional reset button had been successfully pushed. The eventual diagnosis was not paranoia, as my self-evaluation had assumed, but hypervigilance. My layman's understanding of the condition is that it manifests in an intensified state of alertness and an exaggerated need to constantly scan the near environment for possible threats.

In the current vernacular, "hypervigilance" might be described as "situational awareness" on steroids; the difference being, the former is an uncontrolled compulsion acquired from having been in a perpetual state of readiness for an extended period of time, while the latter is a learned response. Situational Awareness is a positive attribute to practice, especially for law enforcement personnel and training in that skill has become a part of police and military instruction as well as civilian Concealed Carry classes.

The above is my interpretation of my diagnosis, in my words, and not in the exact phrasing or terminology of the diagnosis provided by my psychologist.

****

The dreams still occur, albeit less frequently, but I'm in a better place emotionally. In conversations with my "Shrink," as I admiringly and respectfully refer to her, I've learned that not all wounds bleed. Unadmitted and untreated mental and moral wounds can fester unnoticed for years, not unlike an emotional cancer that will eventually exude symptoms.

****

Having begun the repairing process allowed me to understand more fully the mental anguish experienced by my father-in-law, before his passing in 2003.

At the age of 23, he was an officer in a tank destroyer unit during World War II. He was a recipient of the Silver Star for valor in combat as well as the Purple Heart. During the Battle of the Bulge, he was captured and held prisoner by Nazi forces. Along with a few members of his unit, he managed to escape the prison camp, but was eventually recaptured.

After the war, like most veterans of his era, he returned to his work, his church and his family. Like many of his fellow soldiers with similar battle experience, he lived most of his life exhibiting no outward signs of the trauma he had experienced during the war.

When health issues mandated his retirement, and daily responsibilities were no longer a diversion to thinking and remembering, the horrific memories and dreams began haunting him full time. Dementia soon followed his PTSD. On many nights, I was called to his home to sit with him during some frightening hallucinations. During many of the all night sessions I repeatedly attempted to convince him that the war was over, he was safe and, the most challenging, that I wasn't one of his German captors. My efforts sometimes calmed him, but usually ended with him surrendering to exhaustion and sleeping into the following afternoon.

He and his men were immersed daily in the horrors of their war. Blood, death, mutilation and a genuine fear of execution as prisoners-of-war were part of their experience. His was a severe case of PTSD, but identifiable symptoms didn't appear until he was in his seventies and had little to occupy his mind but memories.

****

Writing these pages has been an intermittent effort over a period of ten years. At first it was a rewarding task and quite enjoyable. As the writing progressed into recording my military adventures, the enjoyment began to wane.

Countless pages were written, reviewed then torn up. Some content sounded to me like whining –I'm not a whiner. Some sounded too dramatic – drama is not my style. Some bordered on what might be interpreted by a reader as sensationalism. I deplore sensationalism, whether it is in news reporting or exaggerated personal anecdotes. In either case, it is an affront to the listener's intelligence. With the exception of a few passages, I have chosen to exclude details of any graphic violence that lend nothing to my story.

When I began writing about my military years I became more emotional and prone to nightmares again. I attempted to share my feelings with a close friend who gave his opinion freely and succinctly, "Your writing is like picking a scab that's trying to heal."

It seems ironic to me that the very thing (this writing) that caused my memory and emotions to run wild is now being continued as an important part of my therapy!

Addressing my obsession with nighttime security and my tendency to sleep with one eye open led to the acquisition of two intelligent, loving and alert standard poodles – Ollie and Chester. They are my constant companions around the house, whether inside or out, and are sprawled at my feet as I write this. I no longer react to every unidentified noise in the night… that's their job.

Over the past thirty years or so we have adopted several needy dogs from local rescues – many, near the end of their useful lives. In most cases they needed more therapy than I.

Ollie and Chester are the exception to our rescue habit, and they are proving to be able therapists.

My ever vigilant staff

CHAPTER FORTY-THREE

As I review my own words on the preceding pages, two things have become evident that I want to address. The first is that I get the uneasy feeling that some of my thoughts may be misconstrued, particularly with regard to my opinion of military service. It's easy to pick at, and try to expose, the perceived flaws of any organization whether you're a part of it or an outsider where opinions are easily formed from a safe distance. The military, whose ultimate purposes are to wage war, maintain peace and defend our homeland, provides a rich environment for criticism – sometimes based in fact, but often unfounded.

I want to state sincerely and, for the record, that I have nothing but respect and admiration for our military forces past and present; in particular our current branches of service that consist entirely of volunteers. My writing has included accounts of several instances of screw ups, human errors and mistakes that could be part of any normal life regardless of status - military or civilian. Come to think of it, this would have been a very short story if it didn't include the Army's miscues as well as mine! I'm proud to have served in the military and feel that it was not only a positive, but very necessary part of my life.

Second, much of the first chapter of my book made reference to one of my childhood biblical heroes, David the shepherd boy. The fact that I attempted, usually unsuccessfully, to repeat some of his recorded actions is the reason for the inclusion of his name in the title. After that first chapter, David was relegated to a few cameo references. As mentioned before, I often tried emulating the physical feats attributed to my early idols; many of those attempts ending in near disaster.

It is my contention that kids need heroes or role models to pattern their imaginative play after. Healthy hero worship will usually end when boys notice girls and girls notice boys, or when adulthood replaces playful imagination with societal inflicted sobriety.

I was impressed early on with David's bravery, skill, wisdom and talent, in addition to his unwavering faith in his God. However his story, like that of many other larger than life personalities, provides an important life lesson…every living being has flaws.

When I was about twelve, a well-meaning Sunday school teacher presented me with a book – I think it was a reward for perfect attendance. I don't remember the title, but it was a detailed account of King David. Although I had left my hero worship stage by then, I was thrilled to receive the book.

Had my Sunday school teacher/benefactor been aware of the author's detailed account of my hero's indiscretion with his neighbor's wife, he would have given me a perfect attendance button instead!

Right there, in black and white before my wide, unbelieving eyes was an X-rated, biblical soap opera that couldn't possibly be true. Being on the cusp of adolescence, and somewhat hormone compromised, I reread the account several times - only in the interest of clarity.

Needing verification of the author's outlandish claims, I went to my Bible to fact check the author's story. There it was in black and white, albeit in smaller print. The shocking truth!

My childhood heroes were taking some serious hits! First the disappointment of Samson's downfall, and now this!

****

In idle moments as a child, and to a lesser extent as an adult, I have often looked for comparisons between my life and those of my childhood heroes, both fictional and real. Thoughts of David were the subject of many of those daydreams.

In most cases the contrasts were more pronounced than

the similarities:

- David was a talented poet, song writer and musician.
- Me, not so much.
- As a shepherd boy, David fashioned his homemade weapons with the materials he had on hand.
- As a child, I fashioned my first bow and quiver of arrows by destroying my mom's lilac bush.
- David volunteered to serve his desperate people by fighting and defeating a dangerous enemy in a decisive battle.
- I volunteered to serve my ideologically divided country in a questionable war that had no resolution.
- David defeated and killed his giant with a homemade sling.
- I held six tiny enemy soldiers at bay with a handgun then ended the confrontation by releasing them.
- David was innately brave and confident.
- What bravery I possess is born of a distaste of fearfulness. What confidence I have, I earned through experience.
- David became King of his people.
- I have no political aspirations.
- David was a valiant warrior who killed thousands of his enemies.
- I was a dutiful soldier, never fired a shot, and was thankful to have my war behind me.
- David had multiple wives and still was guilty of adultery.
- I've been constantly happy, and occasionally overwhelmed, with just one!

Finally, though our lives are separated by distinctly different cultures and several thousand years, David and I are two men apart who are in awe of the same God…

Surely goodness and mercy shall follow me
All the days of my life:
And I will dwell in the house of the Lord
FOR EVER.

Psalms of David 23:6

EPILOGUE

In a nutshell, the past fifty-some years have been filled with more joy and sadness, blessings and tragedies, rewards and losses than can be recalled, but that is the lot of anyone privileged to live long enough to experience life's metaphoric roller coaster.

Sometimes we must accept what fate hands us – sometimes good, sometimes bad. As a free people, living in a free society, we enjoy options that are often denied to people in countless countries around the world. Thankfully, I was blessed to be born in this wonderful country, with good health and an adequate portion of common sense to enjoy those blessings and make my own way in life.

My blessings do not include a vast accumulation of wealth – that just didn't happen. Far more important to my personal enjoyment of life are my family and a few dear friends. To spend my life with a wonderful woman and help in rearing three amazing daughters who married intelligent, faithful husbands, I consider my ultimate blessing. Our daughters have blessed us with two grandchildren each, and are engaged in successful, respected careers. Don't get me started on my grandkids!

I could go on for pages about each of them. It is sufficient to say, I'm blessed.

Made in the USA
Coppell, TX
13 December 2021